University of the Pacific

Sesquicentennial: 1851-2001

STOCKTON

CALIFORNIA

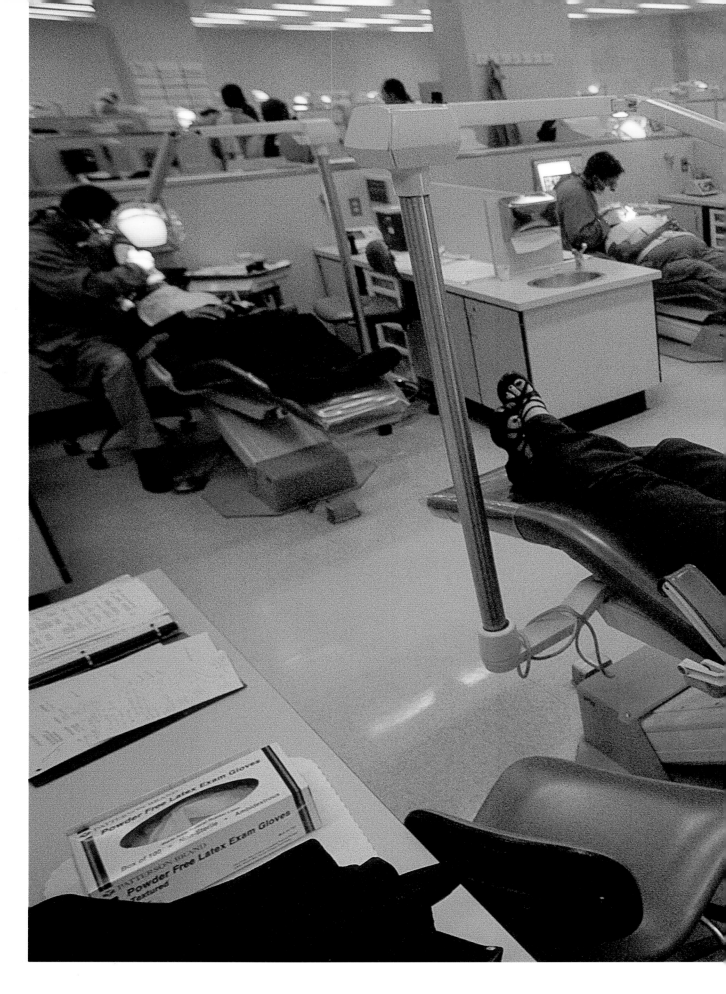

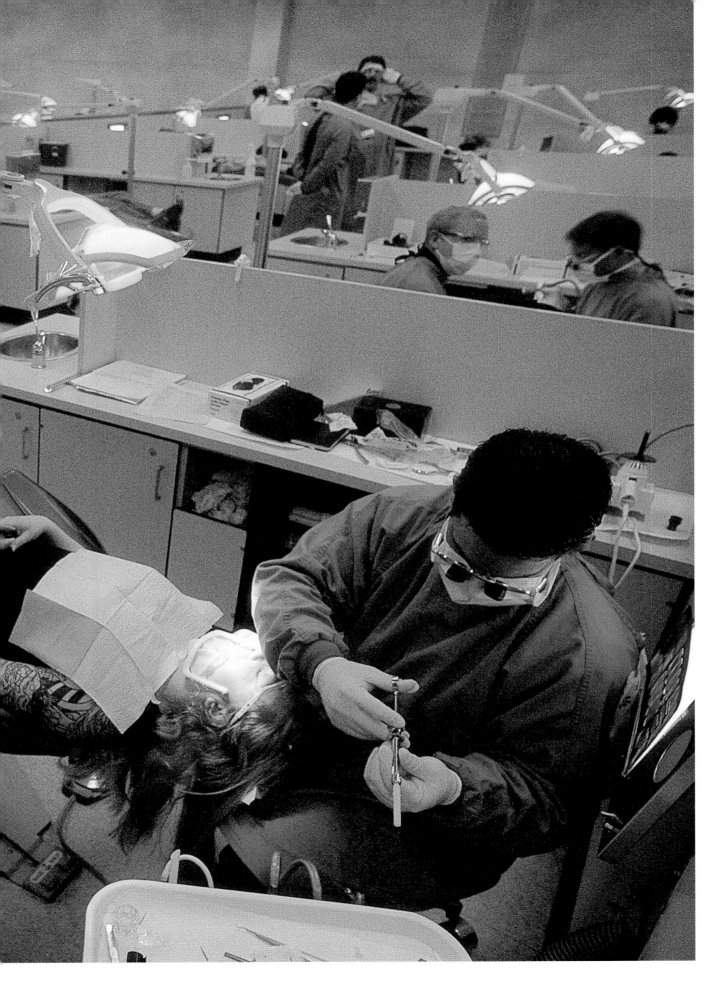

SAN FRANCISCO

SACRAMENTO

Voice Professor Lynelle Wiens and student Keri Klayko. '03.

THE PROFESSOR WHO CHANGED MY LIFE

A sesquicentennial celebration of educational interaction at University of the Pacific

Text by
Charles Clerc

Color Photographs by
James A. Sugar
Corbis

1851-2001

Harmony House Publishers

Executive Committee for the Sesquicentennial Anniversary

Editor: Russell L. Wylie
Assistant Vice President
Marketing and University Relations

Author: Charles Clerc, Ph.D.
Professor Emeritus
University of the Pacific

Color Photography: James A. Sugar

Historic Photos:* William Knox Holt
Memorial Library Holt-Atherton Special
Collection

Design: Boz Johnson

Editorial Advisory Board:
Kara Brewer
Leslie Crow
Dan Kasser
Todd Ruhstahler
Don Walker*

*The staff wishes to extend special appreciation
to Pacific Archivist Don Walker for his skills in
searching for historical photographs.

Published by:
University of the Pacific in association with
Harmony House Publishers - Louisville
P.O. Box 90 Prospect, Kentucky 40059
502-228-2010
William Strode: Editor

Archival Photography:
University of the Pacific Archives
Color Photography © by James A. Sugar,
2001

Library of Congress Number 00-108196
Hardcover International Standard
Book Number 1-56469-077-6

Charter Sponsors

The Regents, staff, faculty and students of Pacific express their appreciation for the generosity of alumni and friends who, as Charter Sponsors, made possible the planning and preparation of the Sesquicentennial Anniversary.

Individuals

Bill L. Atchley
Pat Atchley
Honoring Jennifer Lee Atwood (2001)
Dr. James DeHaven Atwood
Walter A. Baun (1953)
Betty Baun
Marrino Berbano (1957)
Mary Berbano
Judge William Biddick, Jr. (1941)
Dorothy Biddick (1945)
Virginia Weston Blewett (1939)
Robert N. Blewett
Mark Jon Bluth (1978)
Jonathan A. Brown (1968)
Quinlan Brown (1968)
David W. Brubeck (1942)
Iola Brubeck (1945)
Jeanne C. Burbank (1950)
Patrick D. Cavanaugh
Janita Cavanaugh
Dr. Judith M. Chambers (1958)
Dr. Dewey Chambers
Dr. Norman C. Chapman (1946)
Dorothy M. Chapman
Clay Clement (1965)
Dr. D. Clifford Crummey (1934)
Joan Darrah (1974)
James P. Darrah
Erma DeCarli (1936)
Dean DeCarli
Dorothy de la Cruz-Schmedel (1989)
Wayne de la Cruz-Schmedel
Dr. Donald V. DeRosa
Karen M. DeRosa
Dr. Arthur A. Dugoni (1948)
Katherine A. Dugoni
Frank D. Fargo
Marian R. Fargo
Frances Korbel Ferguson
Joseph H. Friedrich
Sheila R. Friedrich
David Gerber (1950)
Laraine Gerber
Philip N. Gilbertson
Carole P. Gilbertson
Steven J. Goulart (1980)
Kristy Courtland Goulart (1979)
Ralph Guild (1950)
Calla Murphy Guild
Bob Hanyak (1979)
Martha Cassidy Hanyak (1978)

Catherine R. Harnack (1941)
Rolando A. Hermoso (1976)
Sheryl L. Keith (1977)
Steve L. Hunton
Carolee Hunton
E. Pendleton James (1954)
Betty James
Kathleen Lagorio Janssen (1968)
Dean Janssen (1968)
James Earl Jewell (1951)
Senator Patrick Johnston
Margaret M. Johnston
Raoul D. Kennedy (1964)
Patricia A. Kennedy (1966)
Howard M. Koff
Marcia Koff
Evelyn L. Lagorio
Janice D. Magdich (1979)
James D. Mair (1968)
Gretchen W. Mair (1968)
Jesse J. Marks, Jr. (1965)
Professor Elizabeth Matson
A. Russell McPherson (1930)
Honor McPherson
Jonathan Meer
Robert T. Monagan, Jr. (1942)
Margaret Ione Monagan (1945)
Weldon T. Moss (1963)
Elaine Moss
Mike Minoru Namba (1985)
Dr. Vance C. R. Nelson (1957)
Robin J. Nelson (1957)
Phap D. Nguyen
Marie Nguyen
Robert F. Nikkel (1942)
Marge Nikkel
Donald E. O'Connell
Carol O'Connell
Kelli Williams Page (1987)
Betty Jo Peterson (1954)
Dianne L. Philibosian (1968)
Thomas D. Seifert
Jerrald K. Pickering (1953)
Frances A. Pruner
David K. Rea
Elizabeth H. Rea
William A. Richardson (1969)
Linda Richardson
Diane Rulnick
Edgar Sanderson
James P. Sargen
Joan Sargen

Ralph L. Saroyan (1964)
Honoring Brice D. Schilling (2000)
John R. Schilling, APC
Marian V. Schroven (1929)
Arnold C. Scott (1939)
Barbara P. Sheldon
Dr. Kok-Chun Si-Hoe
Choon Lian Tan Si-Hoe
Donald J. Smith (1952)
Doenda Hammond Smith (1952)
A. Edward Spiegel
Shondell Spiegel
Lee Stafko
Joan Stafko
John R. Stein
Cathy Stein
Preston Thompson
Joanne Thompson
Janet Korn Valenty (1967)
Bonnie Gottlieb Vistica (1975)
Jack F. Vogel (1947)
Eleanor M. Vogel (1945)
Robert L. Wicker (1935)
Margaret E. Wicker
Dr. Robert R. Winterberg (1951)
Patricia Winterberg (1950)
Frank C. Wood (1938)
Jeaneva L. Wood
Rob M. Wooton (1971)
Jody R. Wooton
Russell L. Wylie
Marilyn A. Wylie
Dr. Herbert K. Yee (1948)
Inez Ruth Yee
Peter H. Zischke
Marian Zischke

Corporations and Foundations

AAA - California State Automobile
  Association
Capecchio Foundation
  Joan A. Cortopassi (1958)
  Dean A. Cortopassi
Pacific Gas and Electric Company
Peninsula Community Foundation
  Louise Karr (1965)
  Howard Karr
San Francisco Foundation
  Fillmore C. Marks (1951)
  Barbara Marks

McGeorge School of Law Professor Kojo Yelpaala

Contents

Karen Satterly Bensch, McGeorge '02

Foreword

On July 10, 1851, the Supreme Court of California in session in Sacramento issued to University of the Pacific the state's first charter authorizing and recognizing an institution of higher learning. In celebrating that event of 150 years ago and the ensuing history and the promising future that beckons, we present this book as a keepsake that chronicles the university's pioneering past and presents a prospectus for the 21st century.

The book's title *The Professor Who Changed My Life* reflects what has been and will continue to be distinctive about Pacific: higher education that is student centered. The learning process is achieved through close and intense interaction between teacher and student. In an age in which higher education is dominated by research universities and large lecture halls and impersonal TV outlets, Pacific continues to offer education as it was intended when students gathered with Socrates at the agora in classical times or today when they gather around a laptop computer in Professor John Livesey's pharmacy classroom or debate an ethical issue in Professor Jim Heffernan's frosh Mentor Seminar. This education strives to train the whole person through membership in a tightly knit community of teacher-scholars and student-scholars.

We have therefore chosen to mark our Sesquicentennial by celebrating the transformations that take place in young lives through our kind of education. This volume testifies that Pacific's student-centered faculty, during 150 years of service, fulfilled the institution's highest ideals by having prepared graduates for lasting achievement and responsible leadership in their careers and communities.

Donald V. DeRosa

President

January 1, 2001

Megan Burnham '02 enthusiastically participates in October's Midnight Madness.

Reflections

While it may chronicle events, building construction, a mix of personalities, this narrative can in no way capture the intangibles that make up university life: the click and snap of ideas being exchanged in a classroom, over a conference table, within a residence hall.

The intensity of an intramural sport can crackle no less than a tied score, with runners on base, in the last inning of a women's championship softball game. Both are palpable but immeasurable. Nor can the narrative capture the gratification that comes from mastery of a demanding calculus problem; the frustration that results from an elusive scientific experiment; the anxiety caused by a term paper that insists upon further revision.

It cannot capture the elation of that hard-earned *A*, the satisfaction of that *B*, the shrug at the ordinary *C*, the disappointment of that unexpected *D*, and an *F*—enough said.

No narrative can encapsulate the socializing in a sorority den, along a campus walkway, between events at a swim meet, over computer terminals at the library. It's impossible to capture the knowing but repressed smile when a wise professor recognizes that a couple—new to class and new to each other—have somehow—just like that!—joined for life.

It cannot record the comic snore of a seeing-eye dog in a classroom aisle; it can't paint the kaleidoscope of snazzy costumes on the night of Band Frolic; it can't feel old-time slimy slides on water-soaked lawns; it can't taste the punch bowl at a campus party; it can no longer smell the cannon shot fired after touchdowns at Stagg Memorial Stadium—ours, not theirs.

But it can try. That's what narratives are: attempts to re-create. And pictures are the handmaidens. As the Chinese proverb goes: "One picture is worth more than ten thousand words." The number might be debated, but not the impact.

Burns Tower

In the early period of Pacific's move to Stockton in the 1920s began the landscaping, the planting of trees, flowers, bushes that in their luxuriant variety distinguish the main campus today. In fact, four oaks still thriving along Pacific Avenue sprang up as saplings in the Jazz Age. Fifty species of trees were planted, including sequoias, cypress, cedars, firs, junipers, sycamores, oriental cherry, eucalyptus. Ivied walls provide a backdrop for dozens of varieties of blooming flowers, plants, and bushes. A stroll through the central campus rose garden when it's at resplendent full bloom would satisfy even the most discriminating of flower lovers. Kudos go to the landscape architects and gardeners who have created and maintained such serene beauty. The appeal of the landscaping and ivied brick buildings has proven magnetic for Hollywood movie makers. They have used campus settings on numerous occasions for films such as *RPM*, *The Sure Thing*, *Dreamscape*, and *Raiders of the Lost Ark*.

CHAPTER ONE

THE PROFESSOR WHO CHANGED MY LIFE

We dedicate our Commemoration not to bricks, not to presidents and deans or other notables, but to the teachers and to their students for whom "higher learning" has been life transforming.

Professor Claude Rohwer (right) counsels first-year contract students at McGeorge.

A mistaken notion guided young Dave Brubeck's first years at Pacific: that he ought to pursue a major in veterinary science.

His science teacher knew better.

"Brubeck," the professor said, "your mind is not on cutting up frogs. Go across the lawn next year to the Conservatory because that's where your mind is. It's not in the lab."

"I did that, and it changed my life completely."

The rest is musical history. Dave Brubeck, a graduate of the Conservatory in 1942, told his story in those words at Pacific's 2000 Commencement. There he became the first recipient of a California Gold Medal, for his significant contributions to jazz, to composition, and to music in general around the world. His wife, Iola Whitlock Brubeck, a 1945 Pacific graduate and a noted librettist and lyricist, received an honorary doctorate in humane letters at the same convocation.

The Brubecks and President Don DeRosa, May 2000

A university exists to develop the mind of each student. Yes, spirit and body, too, but with solitariness and socialization, the simple process of teaching-learning, of learning-teaching matters most. Students learn from their teachers, and to a surprising degree teachers learn from their students. This reciprocity pumps the heart and fuels the brain of higher education. Its courses of action are centuries long and never-ending: thinking, inquiring, probing, creating, writing, articulating, building, investigating, solving, imagining, assimilating, inventing, inspiring.

For this memorial book, alumni of University of the Pacific were asked to write about professors who influenced them most profoundly. What did those professors do to shape them as human beings? to alter them as students? to affect their careers? to change their lives? And why?

The strand that runs through all of the following stories is *caring*... teachers who cared about their students. These professors loved teaching, but added an extra dimension: personal attention to their students. The caring rubbed off, held, stuck; the Pacific experience became paramount.

CHARLES HAMILTON

For example, Lloyd Teel, class of 1950, now a resident of Modesto, California, remembers most of Pacific's "numerous great teachers." But one in particular, Charles Hamilton, in Education, stood out from the beginning. Teel came to Pacific as a Navy veteran, married, and with a young daughter. Due to a tight schedule of studies and an outside job, he had to wear work clothes to class, thus setting him apart from the others. "On the first exam Dr. Hamilton gave, I received the highest score. It was difficult for him to believe that this poorly dressed student who usually sat near the front row could 'cool' his test." The professor checked out his transcript and called him into his office for a conference. They became friends, and he helped guide Teel's educational pursuits:

He was instrumental in my becoming president of the Student Teacher's Association. I remember on numerous occasions Dr. Hamilton would meet with a group of us at a restaurant or even at his home where we would discuss educational philosophy and other matters related to teaching. I sometimes thought I learned more from those informal meetings than I did in class. Upon graduation he provided me with outstanding recommendations. I believe all this describes an individual who was caring, took an interest in his students beyond just the classroom, and invested himself in their future. He was a truly dedicated teacher, one I will never forget.

Teel

I sometimes thought I learned more from those informal meetings than I did in class.

Professor Jessica Flores helps as a Speech-Language Pathology student learns to give children hearing tests.

FELIX A. WALLACE

Stephen H. Goodman of Campbell, California, who earned a B.S. in 1949, praises Professor Felix A. Wallace, freshly appointed chair of a new Engineering program.

The engineering classes were very small, which made the faculty readily available for individual instruction when needed. We had several dinner parties at our professors' homes. Dr. Wallace personally arranged and accompanied members of the student engineering society on field trips to civil engineering projects and activities. I remember in particular his attending a semester-ending picnic of the society at Louis Park and 'having a beer' with his students. During my senior year at Pacific, Dr. Wallace was assigned the task of designing and managing construction of the present football stadium. I remember being part of a team of engineering students working on the stadium's design under his guidance. Thanks to Dr. Wallace, I was able to use the education represented by my degree to become a certified professional engineer and experience a rewarding career in civil engineering.

Goodman

The engineering classes were very small, which made the faculty readily available for individual instruction when needed.

G. WARREN WHITE

In commenting on the importance of mathematics, Patricia White Sprague, B.A., 1950, from La Jolla, California, quotes the 13th century English philosopher and scientist Roger Bacon: "For he who knows not mathematics cannot know any other science; what is more, he cannot discover his own ignorance or find its proper remedy." She continues: "Mathematics touches us all, and often a professor touches us even more."

He helped us to learn how to distinguish right from wrong, and take the proper path.

Many outstanding teachers do much more than merely "teach." They provide the opportunity, the encouragement, the example for their students to "learn" in and out of the classroom. As a professor of Mathematics at Pacific for 44 years, G. Warren White epitomizes this gift. He made the use of numbers seem real and important and helped us focus on learning. One of his most useful classes was "Principles of Investments," which brought special meaning to students on how to make the best use of whatever funds they might have, a concept that bodes well for the remainder of one's life. He helped us to learn how to distinguish right from wrong, and take the proper path. To use mathematics as a force, not just rote remembering. To use studies as a way for self-improvement, to look at all aspects of life as a wonderful learning experience which should be treasured. His legacy continues through the G. Warren White and Ruby Zahn White scholarship fund at Pacific and placement of his name on the campus entrance gate on Pershing (at Alpine).

JOHN CRABBE

Stanley Lichtenstein, B.A., 1949, of Alameda, California, fondly remembers John Crabbe, director of radio:

...he created in his students a desire to learn...

John Crabbe was the perfect teacher. He mastered his subject completely, and he created in his students a desire to learn and to succeed in Broadcasting. He was responsible for bringing to Stockton one of the first FM radio stations in the area and staffing with college students ready for the challenge. He encouraged us to go beyond the station format and to present college sports, other campus programs, and remote activities. The proof of John's ability can be found in the quality of students he sent into communications, broadcasting, and entertainment: Ralph Guild, Daren F. McGavren, David M. Gerber, Harry Martin Uhlenberg, Clare Rampton, and Don Rodewald. John was not only a great teacher and advisor, he always had time for a student's personal problem. He was the consummate educator and a warm friend.

Lichtenstein

It so happens that John Crabbe, who earned both B.A. (1937) and M.A (1940) at Pacific, met an undergraduate named Bobbin Gay Peck at Pacific Little Theater. They later married and in 2000 celebrated their 60th anniversary. In her tribute to her husband and to drama director DeMarcus Brown, Bobbin Gay (Peck) Crabbe, (B.A. 1938, M.A., 1941) of Sacramento, declares, "Yes, Pacific definitely changed my life."

DEMARCUS BROWN

In a similar vein, Lois LaBonte, B.M., 1957, a professional singer and dancer from Encino, California, lauds DeMarcus Brown, "among many outstanding Pacific teachers":

He stands out in my memory as having been instrumental in shaping my entire future. It was he who had faith in my talent and cast me as the female lead, Lola Pratt, in the musical "Seventeen," while I was still a mere sophomore. His faith gave me the encouragement and impetus to pursue a professional singing career, which I enjoyed for most of my adult life. He also surprised me backstage one night at the Curran Theatre in San Francisco when I was appearing with either Tammy Grimes in "The Unsinkable Molly Brown" or Carol Channing in "Hello Dolly" (I've forgotten which). I owe a debt of gratitude to DeMarcus Brown, and his positive influence will never be forgotten by me.

His faith gave me the encouragement and impetus to pursue a professional singing career...

LaBonte

GEORGE COLLIVER

Wanda Galt, B.A, 1950, writes from her home in Fresno that "two teachers at Pacific changed my life: Dr. George Colliver and Dr. Irving Goleman."

IRVING GOLEMAN

They both opened up the world of ideas for me. They asked the Why? What if? How do we know?—questions that started students down their road to discovery of truth and self. Each one, in his own way, introduced us to eternal questions and to the great minds of the past which had wrestled with them. It was a most valuable journey. The quest was a rich and rewarding one, and no student could ever be blessed with better guides than these two men. They taught me to think.

O. H. RITTER

George W. Druliner, B.A., 1947, who lives in Scottsdale, Arizona, names O. H. Ritter:

I used this philosophy through my entire life.

"My accounting instructor taught me how to 'balance the books,' and 'stay out of the red.' I used this philosophy through my entire life." Then he gives credit to tennis coaches Rube Wood and Phil Garlington for teaching him the importance of "scheduling" and "recruiting." As for the latter, Druliner says, "A manager's success is based on the quality of salesmen he selects."

Druliner

27

WILHELMINA HARBERT

Norman C. Chapman of Calabasas, California, who graduated from the Conservatory of Music in 1946, asks, "How do I choose only two faculty members when so many changed my life?" He states that Wilhelmina Harbert "occupies a special place in my memory":

How do I choose only two faculty members when so many changed my life?

> *Known for starting the Music Therapy program at Pacific, she was a delightful teacher. She taught a course called "Social Objectives of Music," which of course we renamed "Social Objections to Music." As part of this course, I started under her direction an instrumental ensemble made up of patients at Stockton Mental Hospital. Students also gave concerts for the patients, and she was very careful about emotional content of our selections. Mrs. Harbert always misplaced her glasses, but her seemingly disorganized style was deceptive. She knew exactly what she was doing, and all of her students gained knowledge directly or by osmosis.*

J. RUSSELL BODLEY

The other faculty member named by Chapman was J. Russell Bodley, who later became Dean of the Conservatory of Music:

> *His passion was the A Cappella Choir, but he was a superb teacher in anything he taught. Some students were intimidated by him, but most were stimulated. As a published choral composer, he was universally respected for his musicianship, and as a choral conductor he had no peer. Unlike others, he did not flay the air, and his beat and hand movements were precise. All in all, I look back on my undergraduate experience at Pacific with happiness and gratitude.*

Another graduate, class of 1954, who wishes to remain anonymous, also includes J. Russell Bodley as one of "two faculty members who were stalwarts of COP in the forties, fifties, and beyond. The other was Harold Jacoby, my major professor. It is not an exaggeration to say that each of them changed my life, in that they believed in me when I did not believe in myself."

> *J. Russell Bodley was, of course, loved by everyone. It was so inspiring to sing under him, and thus be motivated to develop the skills necessary to pass the audition for the A Cappella Choir. Fifty years later I am still a choral singer. More importantly, singing under him and taking choral conducting from him sustained me during a period when I was quite depressed.*

HAROLD JACOBY

Dr. Jacoby's support of me, especially his insistence that I do well academically, allowed me to take my next step after COP into graduate school and subsequently begin a professional career. I had left COP in great discouragement during the Korean War. After my two years of service, Dr. Jacoby welcomed me back and made me get to work. Knowledge of his career—his service at the Tule Lake Japanese-American Relocation Center during World War II and with the United Nations Relief and Rehabilitation Agency in Yugoslavia after the war—helped me. This, I thought, was what a sociologist should do.

LEONARD O'BRYON

Roy O. Williams, B.A., 1964, of Stockton, fondly remembers a language instructor:

Dr. Leonard O'Bryon was one of my role models when I was in college. He was my German teacher. I do not remember the German, as it has been 39 years. What I do remember is his kindness, his quiet leadership, his always being available to help and to encourage me. I did not get particularly good grades, but that was not the purpose of Dr. O'Bryon's teaching. He taught you to listen, to learn, to do your best, also don't expect perfection, but continue to grow.

Williams

I can say without equivocation that Dr. O'Bryon helped me to develop a healthy self-esteem, and he did so by his consistent positive assessment and encouragement. He and his family have remained friends for these 39 years, and although I know they and I miss his wry smile and love, the world is a better place for his being here.

TOM STUBBS

Syd Church, B.A, 1978, who lives in Yorba Linda, California, writes glowingly of Tom Stubbs and Elizabeth Matson, both from Physical Education:

ELIZABETH MATSON

Tom Stubbs changed my life by giving me a chance to go to UOP on a baseball scholarship, combined with other aid and grants. Coming from a very modest family in East Stockton, I couldn't afford to go to college. When I learned that my scholarship covered room and board, I was ecstatic. Living on campus was a great experience, for which I thank Dr. Stubbs with all my heart. He consistently encouraged me to do my best on and off the field. His leadership and guidance have remained with me today. Because of him, I know I am a better dad to my son and daughter.

During my senior year I had the pleasure of taking a class from Libby Matson called "Physical Education for the Handicapped." She was wonderful. I had never met someone who had so much energy and compassion for teaching. When I graduated, I was fortunate to be drafted into minor league baseball. However, I still needed to do my student teaching to receive my teaching credential. No longer on scholarship, I couldn't raise the total tuition for that semester. Libby was my Student Teaching Advisor, and I approached her that fall to tell her I was going to take a year off to save up my money. She told me, "If you don't do it now, you may never do it." She promptly wrote me a check for $1,000, the amount I was short. No questions asked. Remember, this was 1978 dollars and to me a lot of money. I went on to receive my teaching credential, and fifteen months later I paid her back in full. This was the proudest day of my life, and I will be forever grateful to Libby Matson. She is definitely one of a kind.

FRANCIS W. SAYRE

Jeanie (White) Barkett, B.S. 1974, School of Pharmacy, resides in Portland, Oregon. She writes:

Of the many wonderful professors I encountered at the School of Pharmacy, I need to honor Dr. Francis W. (Frank) Sayre, who changed my professional life.

The first time I saw him I was scared to death. I was a young and skinny woman then, and Dr. Sayre was a tall big man with a strong jaw and wide forehead. His intelligence was formidable, and obviously I was going to be in trouble in his class.

Biochemistry struck fear in all of us. Dr. Sayre was an exacting teacher who demanded the best. A half effort wouldn't be tolerated. Even when I was wailing "I'll never get this," he was always available for one-on-one tutoring, study sessions, explanations, and cheerleading. His enthusiasm for his subject made the difference for me. He loved chemistry only a little more than he loved teaching. His greatest joy was to help a student succeed, and his greatest heart-break (I learned only later) was to watch a student choose to fail.

Well, I didn't become a biochemist, even though I took another class from him as an elective. Dr. Sayre shared his zest for learning that was infectious. It was after I became a pharmacist that I appreciated his passion for his craft.

I had no idea that the teacher I admired was truly a Renaissance Man. He quietly shared his love for music (he sang opera) and poetry after long study/help sessions. He allowed a glimpse of the depth of the man when he revealed that he "went to the Grove" and spent artistic, intellectual, and even patriotic renewal with his bohemian colleagues. Years later he generously shared some of his original poems with me.

It was a sad day when I learned that my mentor and friend had passed. It seems fitting that I'm given the opportunity to eulogize this remarkable man. Somehow I've come full circle to honor him. I now teach. I want to be Dr. Sayre in the eyes of my students: enthusiastic, inspirational, and intelligent. It's a difficult challenge, but one I welcome.

His greatest joy was to help a student succeed...

Barkett

A study session in the library's Information Commons.

ROBERT DASH

In more recent times, Janine Wolf-Henry, B.A., 1986, of Merced, California, even remembers a first conversation with Robert Dash, teacher of Spanish in the Modern Languages Department, that became "pivotal to my future." Lacking confidence in her status in an advanced Spanish class, she consulted with her professor who gave her the encouragement she needed to stay on:

Eventually, I went on to add Spanish as a second major to my International Studies major, and I spent the first semester of my junior year in Madrid, Spain. Dr. Dash was my major advisor, and he also helped prepare me for my time in Spain, not only academically, but, also, culturally. At the end of my college career, I was honored when he presented me with the award for outstanding graduating senior for the Spanish major. Ironically, the skill I was most insecure about all those years ago is now the one I use the most. I work for the Social Security Administration as a bilingual claims representative using Spanish on an almost daily basis.

Wolf-Henry

PAUL GROSS

George J. Buse, who earned his B.S. degree from COP in 1998, praises Dr. Paul Gross of the Chemistry Department, whom he had at first acknowledged "immaturely as 'the professor of pain.'"

The more I listened to Dr. Gross... ...the more I appreciated him.

The more I listened to Dr. Gross—be it in lecture, during office hours, in lab, or at the dinner table—the more I appreciated him. His ideologies were intriguing, his genuine demeanor was conciliating—he made me learn as well as laugh. Two of his most important lessons have catalyzed the formation of my own life principles, #1: True happiness comes from within yourself, and #2: Keep your life in balance. The second resulted after earning an academic award my senior year when Dr. Gross told me something that has been printed indelibly in my mind: 'You're never as good as they say. You're never as bad as they say.' When we were preparing for his difficult exams, Dr. Gross comforted us by saying, 'Focus on 100% perfection as your reference point.' I concluded that the quality of your life is based on your perspective of life; it's all about attitude. Dr. Gross was a great professor as well as an exemplary human being, and I thank him for his guidance and friendship.

DAVID FLETCHER

Dave W. Bass, a graduate of the School of Engineering in the 1980s, tells this incisive, revealing story:

Dr. David Fletcher could strike fear into engineering students attempting to pass his Mechanics of Materials class. I was quite certain he really didn't like young engineering students and was doing all he could to weed them out. Two weeks before Christmas in 1983 I was nearing the end of my first semester with the Wrath of Fletcher. As I was coming out of K-mart, I noticed a group of musicians huddled near the Salvation Army donation pot. I thought my eyes were playing tricks on me. Standing there was Dr. Fletcher, trumpet raised to his pursed lips. Masterfully and passionately he played Christmas carols that warmed the hearts of passers by. Mine was no exception.

Masterfully and passionately he played Christmas carols that warmed the hearts of passers by.

BOB ORPINELLA

Greg Acciaioli, a university professor in western Australia, attended Raymond College in 1976 before going on to graduate elsewhere. He fervently remembers Bob Orpinella, his philosophy teacher at Raymond:

I wouldn't be out here in Perth trying to teach anthropology to Generation Xers were it not for the example he set of honest and committed teaching. He contributed greatly to my intellectual and moral growth. I have never felt as intellectually challenged as when I was taking his philosophy course, stretching myself to my limits to understand such figures as Wittgensttein and Whitehead. In writing analyses such as on Dewey's Reconstruction in Philosophy I learned more than from any other writing endeavors of my life. Along with the life of the mind, I learned to value collegiality. He convinced me to go on a weekend camping trip with some other students. I still appreciate that concern for my overall welfare. Here, we try to foster among ourselves and our students a sense of humanity, not only aiming to understand but also helping to instill humane social relationships, informed by tolerance and mutuality, as the ultimate goal of anthropology, intellectually and emotionally. That was the sense I got from him above all as a teacher.

I have never felt as intellectually challenged...

RAY SYLVESTER

Susan McDonald Pohorski, B.A., 1977, who now resides in Wisconsin, expresses gratitude for "many things about my time at UOP" and for "the many professors that made it such a great experience." She singles out Ray Sylvester from the School of Business, one of her professors in a paired marketing geology course called "The Business of Energy" in the I & I program for freshmen. His helpfulness, concern, and professionalism changed her goals the very day that she expressed interest in the business field at a conference with him:

It also illustrates the beauty of a small learning community like Pacific.

To my surprise, he took a piece of paper out of his desk, put my name at the top, and listed courses I should take to get a degree in business. When I expressed my fear of math, he reassured me, "From what I've seen of you in class, I think you can handle it." First I was impressed that he knew who I was; second, that he had observed my abilities; third, that he took the time to draw up and explain an academic plan for me. That night I wrote my parents telling them that Pacific was worth every penny in tuition, and that I needed that kind of attention and encouragement. Afterward, I took on a double major in business and communication arts, aiming for a career in public relations. Internships with the Pacific Public Relations office and the Lodi Public Schools helped confirm my decision. I have told this story often because it is so significant in my life. It also illustrates the beauty of a small learning community like Pacific.

McGeorge Professor Gregory Webster

CORT SMITH

"The real voyage of discovery consists not in seeing new landscapes, but in having new eyes. While somewhat trite, Marcel Proust's observation actually does remind me of Professor Cort Smith." So writes Thomas M. Miller, B. A., 1985, of San Francisco. He adds:

His insights were piercing, his knowledge extensive, and his use of language profound.

Cort Smith stands out above all other teachers in influencing my life. His influence began with Introduction of Political Science—taken my freshman year—and extended into my senior year in which he served as professor, advisor, and friend. His insights were piercing, his knowledge extensive, and his use of language profound. His influence contributed to my decision to study abroad, to immerse myself in other cultures, and, ultimately, to pursue a consulting career that has spanned three continents. To this day, few people I have known possess the combination of lucid intellect, skillful communication, and passion for learning that Cort Smith does. For me, he set the standard for outstanding teaching and global citizenship. As a result of his influence, I have in fact gone on to see many new landscapes. But most importantly, thanks to Cort Smith, I have the eyes to appreciate and better understand what I am seeing.

RUFO LOPEZ-FRESQUET

Haino Burmeister, B. A., 1973, Covell College, who resides in Sao Paulo, Brazil, hearkens back to an incident involving Rufo Lopez-Fresquet, Professor of Economics at Covell College during the 1970s. He explains that Professor Lopez-Fresquet "had been Minister of Finance during the first 14 months of Fidel Castro's government in Cuba and fled to the USA when communism dominated the island." He describes the professor as "a citizen of the world, highly educated, well traveled. He knew and loved human beings as few are able to do. With his long, white, curly hair he resembled an orchestra conductor. He loved to be at the Covell Center, among students, talking about anything from baseball to politics, historical and contemporary issues to his beloved Cuba. Everything about Professor Lopez-Fresquet could be learned from his conduct once at the Covell Center":

One night in 1972 he made a presentation during a homecoming seminar on current issues and strongly criticized the Cuban government. After he had finished his talk, a young man with a shaven head stood up at the rear of the full audience and in a controlled manner criticized every point made by the speaker. The young man had just returned from Cuba where he had done volunteer work with the "Brigada Venceremos," he had first-hand experience in Cuba, his points were made to discredit the old man. At the end of his diatribe, a long silence followed— breaths were held in expectation of how Professor Lopez-Fresquet would respond. Those of us who did not know the young man feared the worst; the old professor could be sarcastic and contemptuous when confronted by ignorance or ill intention. Instead, Professor Lopez-Fresquet answered in a modulated tone. He said that probably people in the audience would be perplexed by his son's statements. He said there wasn't anything to be argued in public that had not already been argued at home. He said life was that way and he accepted it, as he accepted his son's right to take an opposite position, but he could not agree with his son's opinions. This was Rufo Lopez-Fresquet: fiery but fair-minded, a man who could keep in balance his emotional and cerebral reactions. I learned much that night about tolerance, flexibility, savoir faire, and human relations.

...a man who could keep in balance his emotional and cerebral reactions.

Sarah Tompkins '03 is challenged by a temporary wall.

DEWEY CHAMBERS

Greta Meyer, B.A. 1966, a resident of Stockton, recalls Dr. Dewey Chambers from the year when she was completing her teaching credential at the School of Education:

In the classroom, he was knowledgeable and interesting, with a great sense of humor

Meyer

He was an enthusiastic young man, friendly, free and easy, enjoying life (including, as he told us, spending weekends on the ocean with his surfboard). In the classroom, he was knowledgeable and interesting, with a great sense of humor. His lectures were well prepared, thorough, packed with information, and always entertaining. We all knew, even back then, of his gifts as a storyteller. He had a way with children's stories that was truly fascinating. I remember that he was not a great fan of Disney movies and didn't think much of Disney's characters. Neither did I. He much preferred the power of books for children over any movie, because of their appeal to the imagination. As mother and teacher who knew the importance of books and stories to be read to children and read by children, I came to agree wholeheartedly with him. I also know that he continued onward for many years as an outstanding teacher.

JERALD 'JERRY' NELSON

Marvin E. Locke, Ed.D., 1971, a retired Superintendent of Schools from Red Bluff, California, writes: "As a graduate student at UOP over thirty years ago, I was impressed with the quality and dedication of those professors with whom I studied. Dean Marc Jantzen made it a point to ensure that we were exposed to a broad spectrum of people from many departments in Education; virtually all of them were memorable to me in some positive way":

One person stands out as opening intellectual 'doors' for me. My exposure to research techniques and to statistical analysis in an advanced seminar changed all my previous thinking. The professor was Dr. Jerald 'Jerry' Nelson. He had a humorous, whimsical manner of presentation, using practical examples from the world around us. All of a sudden, the power of statistical analysis became very real. He encouraged us to look at how statistical analyses could be used in a broad array of disciplines. Once he took us to U.C. Davis to show us how these methods could be applied to agriculture, veterinary medicine, and other sciences. Although I am not a mathematician or statistician, I have used his realistic, down-to-earth concepts continually in my professional career as an educator.

Stacy Swofford (right) '01, Carol White '01, and Kelly O'Conner '01

Alec Torres gets 'floor time' while dad Troy Torres '02 studies.

PATTY PIERCE

The Department of English in COP received a sizable share of paeans to influential teachers, ranging all the way from the 1940s into the 1990s.

Eloine Ralph, B.A., l949, writes from her home in Berkeley, California, that Patty Pierce profoundly influenced her life and her career as a technical coordinator in the UC Lawrence Lab:

She opened her home, head, and heart to us

Ralph

When Patty Pierce taught her class, The Development of the English Novel, back in 1948-49, there were no usable textbooks available on that subject. She would enthusiastically research and share her knowledge of these authors from the 18th century into modern times. She worked us hard by having us read 12 big novels and write and present detailed reports. This applied to a Drama course, as well. Also she invited us to her home for lively games of Charades. As she opened her home, head, and heart to us, she opened the world of drama and English literature to me.

ARLEN J. HANSEN

Jeffrey Bartlett, B.A., 1972, now residing in Berkeley, California, says: "Arlen J. Hansen, a professor of English in COP, was one of the two most important mentoring figures in my life after I left home." He recalls first meeting him in the office of the department chairman, who asked "what courses I intended to take as a change of major. When I mentioned that one of them was Modern British and American Fiction, the tall blond man sitting beside the chairman shook his head and said, 'Oh I wouldn't take that one.' When I asked why not, he replied, 'I'm teaching it.' This wry remark ensured that I would take the class."

Bartlett

Arlen's guidance influenced the course of my life. He helped me to get into graduate school at the University of Iowa, where I wrote a Ph.D. dissertation with the noted Americanist Sherman Paul (the other of the two most important men), who had also directed Hansen's dissertation.

Over the years we remained in touch. He read my manuscripts and wrote numerous letters of recommendation. But as well as being a decisively helpful advisor, Arlen was one of the most fun people I've ever known. We and our wives shared many good times; some of the best were in Europe, where both Arlen and I taught on Fulbright fellowships in the mid 1980s Sadly, during that time abroad the first signs appeared of the cancer that eventually took his life. In the remaining seven years, Arlen battled his disease with every medical resource that doctors could suggest and his own indomitable spirit. He even found the strength to write his second book, Gentlemen Volunteers, which was published posthumously

But this is not a sad story. Rather, to remember Arlen is to celebrate him and the pleasure of having known him. At Christmas 1993, a few months after his death, a group of family members, colleagues, and friends all traveled to Paris. There we scattered his ashes in Pere Lachaise Cemetery, where many famous literary figures he had written about are buried.

Our memory of him is embodied in the name of my son, John Arlen Bartlett, born in 1991. Knowing Arlen Hansen surely improved my life. I miss him all the time.

CHARLES CLERC

Leslie New Kranz, B.A., 1976, English and Theatre major, writes from her California home that "although I fondly recall many teachers from various departments there is one whose influence has guided me for, lo, these 24 years":

Here was an instructor willing to challenge, rather than indulge

Dr. Charles Clerc's notes on my first submission in his creative writing class were not encouraging. Essentially, he told me to toss it and 'get down to some bona fide writing.' I remember embarrassment, but far greater was a sense of elation. Here was an instructor willing to challenge, rather than indulge, the flowery prose that had impressed high school teachers. His comments on subsequent writings—both creative and critical—were lengthy and thorough. He helped me recognize grammatical shortcomings, 'little darlings,' incomplete characters, and unfinished thoughts. He taught me to pare and to 'render,' and—most valuable of all—to write clearly. My professional work since has required writing of my own, as well as rewriting the words of others. Through the years, I found Dr. Clerc guiding me still, as I rephrased a sentence or reorganized a paper. All my professors helped shape me in some way, but I credit Dr. Clerc with awakening me to my writing potential. His encouragement and support will last me a lifetime.

RUTH FAUROT

Maureen Guerrero-Null, who took a B. S. degree in the 1960s, writes from Santa Barbara, California, "I am thrilled to be offering my memory of one of the most influential people who ever touched my life: Dr. Ruth Faurot."

I can still see her—about 5' tall, striking gray hair, and a sharp wit. We were addressed as 'Mr.' or 'Miss,' the classroom door was shut at 9:10 sharp [and locked] so that if you were late you missed the class, and if she called on you for a response and you hadn't read the text you were asked to leave. This may sound impossible by today's standards, but in the semesters I took her classes, it was like food to me. She had such a love and knowledge of her subject that Shakespeare became a familiar friend and a lifelong companion. Our coverage and reading of plays was thought-provoking, humorous, and enlightening. The words I had read as a young girl became beautiful music and pleasurable poetry. This was a love that followed me all the stages of my life.

Guerrero-Null

For women graduating in 1965 the world gave us an arc of choices, and the changes in society were turbulent, but through all my 'lives' as career girl, hippie, single mom, recent wife (hard to believe, I know, but I met my husband-to-be in an adult education Shakespeare class in Santa Barbara), my Hardin-Craig edition of Shakespeare plays and my fond memories of Dr. Faurot helped sustain me.

MAURICE McCULLEN

Lori J. Carlson Andrews, B.A., 1984, International Studies (along with her husband John G. Andrews, B.A., 1985, International Studies) from their home in Westport, Connecticut, name three influential teachers, the first of whom is Maurice McCullen, Professor of English. Lori writes:

Maurie encouraged me to stretch myself at every opportunity.

Maurie, my English advisor, was the essence of everything I loved about UOP. His office in Knoles Hall was straight out of a Woody Allen movie—cluttered to the window ledges, maybe even further, dust resting on hundreds of books, and a permanently stained coffee mug. I am a neatnic—but I loved Maurie's office and the way I felt when I was there. It was a sort of organized pandemonium, and it was comforting. Maurie encouraged me to stretch myself at every opportunity. He suggested that I approach The Pacifican *about writing editorials. I did and I got the job. Maurie believed in me so much, and, in turn, that helped me to believe more in myself. Our friendship has continued over the years, and we have gone literally to the ends of the earth to visit one another. When my husband and I lived in London, he visited us; when we lived in Tokyo, he visited us; when he lived in China, we visited him; every time we're in Stockton we have dinner together. I consider Maurie to be one of the persons who has touched my life and made a permanent impression. I deeply thank UOP for such a gift.*

School of Dentistry Dean Arthur Dugoni address students at one of his famous "Brown Bag Lunches."

Pharmacy Professor John Livesey helps Theresa Halperin and Hang Huynh, both '02, with first-year studies.

dy Heide '01 and Marie Cottman '01 help a client during rotations at Green Brothers Pharmacy in Stockton.

DIANE BORDEN

Mary Beth Culp, M.A., 1980, Associate
Professor of English at Marymount College,
Rancho Palos Verdes, California, writes:

*...they provided the foundation
for my view of life's
complexities...*

It's hard to single out any individual from among Pacific's English professors because each of them is special in his/ her own way; however, the unique gifts of Professors Diane Borden and Robert Knighton provided the foundation for my view of life's complexities and the critical faculties that enable me to cope with them.

I'll never forget Dr. Borden's inner illumination as she shared with us her love of film and taught us how to 'read' the movies, a gift I continue to apply to every film I see.

To Dr. Knighton I owe my basic understanding of Existential principles; my personal philosophy, at best fragmentary when I started at Pacific, was forged in the crucible of his classes in Existential Fiction and Literary Criticism. To this day when I'm tempted to write off a decision by saying 'I have no choice,' I think of the antiheroes of Camus, Sartre, Percy, Bellow, and realize that we always have choices, choices that we must make responsibly.

Both Dr. Knighton and Dr. Borden make students want to learn, and it is with great pride that I have evolved from student to colleague, aspiring to continue the tradition of professional excellence that they represent.

ROBERT KNIGHTON

Julianne George Van Leeuwen, B.A. 1981, of
Placerville, California, continues with praise
of Professor Knighton:

From the start I realized that he was a strict disciplinarian—demanding the most from his students. He put his heart and soul into his teaching—his passion for learning, his love of literature were infectious. When I needed his help with assignments, counseling, or direction, he was there for me. Time and again, he spoke to the class as a whole about goal-setting and striving for their attainment. He made us aware of the need for excellence in writing, the importance of correct thinking, the necessity for appreciating the art of reading great books. Dr. Knighton elevated our thinking to the level where we discovered the power and resources of our nature, and began to improve ourselves in order to live with self-esteem and honor. The numerous lessons learned while under his tutelage have helped me to obtain gainful employment, set personal goals, and discover my potential.

*He put his heart and
soul into his teaching...*

Van Leuwen

DONALD DUNS

With similar enthusiasm, Danny T. Dunne, B.A., 1990, M.A, 1993, a Stockton resident and college English instructor, adds laurels for "two men who changed my attitude about myself and also changed the direction of my life forever. I will be eternally grateful for their positive influence, not only with my education, but also the value they put on me as a human being":

One was Dr. Robert Knighton. At our first meeting, his gentle demeanor and flowing white hair made me feel at ease. We struck up a rapport that lasted from that moment through my studies with him to the present day. Nothing ever lifted my spirits as much as his class and his discussions. Nothing has ever inspired me more to continue to read, to satiate my desire for more knowledge, to seek more than I ever had in my entire life. Assisting me through the grueling process of a master's thesis, he spent countless hours going over every page, every paragraph, every sentence, every word, to ensure its accuracy and professionalism. I owe much to his teaching, mentoring, and friendship.

The other was Dr. Donald Duns, the administrator who helped me as I began my educational endeavors later in life than most students. He assured me again and again that my entry into UOP would be a success. Without his words of encouragement, his guidance, his patience, I never would have completed my undergraduate program, much less went on to complete my graduate studies.

He assured me again and again that my entry into UOP would be a success.

Dunne

McGeorge Professor and Associate Dean John Sprankling teaches a first-year property class.

Three briefly mentioned pairings end these shared memories. One comes from Lura Dunn, B.A., 1981, in Seattle, Washington. She says that her Pacific experience in 1979-1981 was made possible by two compassionate professors: Gordon Imlay, who administered an American Humanics program, and Sarah Stebbins, who taught several of its courses. She praises them for "knowing us as people, not as just another student," for being able to confide in them, for "genuinely caring about my situation," and for offering her "an opportunity to develop into the leader that I am today."

Lori J. and John G. Andrews also pair Walter Payne, of Covell College and COP, and Les Robinson, of Covell College. They remember many dinners at the Payne home. "Walter was full of energy and enthusiasm for teaching; he was demanding as a professor and lovable as a friend." As for Dr. Robinson, "he is one of the kindest men we know, and treated students with the utmost respect, in spite of our Blue Books that became seas of red pen. Les Robinson loved red pen. Not only did we benefit from his extensive knowledge, we were also blessed with the friendship of a person who cared deeply about his students."

To Pacific's credit, one former student, Michael M. Arcilla of the Philippines, who attended during the 1980s, spoke appreciatively of assistance given him by two women at the Bechtel Center: Barbara St. Urbain, director of International Services, and her assistant Pam Galbraith. He says that at first he felt overwhelmed as an incoming foreign student, but Ms. St. Urbain and Ms. Galbraith dispelled much of his anxiety. "I can never forget the friendliness and warmth extended to me during orientation. They became my first friends At all times, they made us foreign students feel that we had 'a home away from home.' I am grateful to Barbara and Pam for their support and encouragement."

Sacramento attorney Anthony M. Kennedy served as Adjunct Professor of Constitutional Law at UOP's McGeorge School of Law from the mid 1960s to 1988, when he was appointed Associate Justice of the U.S. Supreme Court, a weighty duty which he has honorably fulfilled since. Despite his busy schedule, Justice Kennedy continues to teach every summer in Salzburg, Austria, at McGeorge's distinctive "Institute on International Legal Studies" that celebrated its 25th anniversary in 1999.

CHAPTER TWO

REMEMBRANCES OF THINGS PAST

Amos Alonzo Stagg, known as the Grand Old Man of Football, came to Pacific in 1933 after retirement from University of Chicago. His teams gained national recognition and a firm and respected place for Pacific in intercollegiate athletics. He introduced into football such innovations as the "T" formation and the forward pass. His devotion to amateur athletics, his unshakable integrity, and his capacity for changing lives (as someone said, helping boys to become men) made him a legendary figure.

For this sesquicentennial celebration, a dozen emeriti faculty and former administrators volunteered comments about their affiliation with the university.

Stan Beckler, composer and music professor, takes pride in the accomplishments of his former students, among them Jamie Horner, Larry Groupe, and Russell Warner, all composers and professional musicians.

Donald H. Grubbs, historian in COP, was considered a radical when he first came to Pacific. To the charge, he bemusedly replies, "I hope I was always worthy of the compliment, since my radicalism derived from the

teachings and actions of people like Jesus of Nazareth and the Founding Fathers."

Marc Jantzen, emeritus dean of the School of Education, enumerates forward strides at the school, like the B.S. in Education with emphasis upon liberal studies, proliferating faculty, the doctorate in education, increased credentialing programs in counseling, school psychology, special education, and administration. He served Pacific for 43 years, which included deanship of Summer Sessions and instigation of Pacific's Music Camp and Folk Dance Camp.

Another administrator, Milton Lambertson, a graduate of COP and former Associate Dean for Financial Services at the School of Dentistry, spent 42 years with the university. He names outstanding people that he knew and worked with: Elliott Taylor, President and Mrs. Burns, Arthur Beckwith, Robert Winterberg, and William Morris, then reserves special praise for Dale Redig and Arthur A. Dugoni at the School of Dentistry. He lauds "Dr. Redig for his whole new philosophy of education, with his development of the humanistic program and change in fiscal

policy." As for Dr. Dugoni, "his personal dedication meant that the professional development of all teachers and administrators was primary." He also stressed that the curriculum of the Dental School had to be "best in the nation, physical facilities must lead in technology, and the humanistic approach to teaching must continue as hallmark of our success." He concludes, "The leadership of Drs. Redig and Dugoni has proven successful with regular superior results in every accreditation, and the school has one of the most positive, supportive alumni in the nation."

Charles D. LaMond, a music professor for 35 years, tells this story: "In the early 1950s, at a concert in the Conservatory, I had to leave my seat and disturb others in the same row, including Amos Alonzo Stagg. 'Will the class of '88 please excuse the class of '38?' I said. (We were both Yalies.) Arising, he smiled. I did not see him again until a week before his death. As I passed the open door to his hospital room, the failing old man (over 100, you know) signaled me to enter and said, ''38, was it?' He smiled again. (And we old codgers think memory dims with age. Ugh.)"

Stanley McCaffrey remembers with fondness enduring friendships at Pacific during his presidency, choosing for specific referral close friends Judith Chambers and Cliff Dochterman. "My seventeen years at Pacific represented one of the most satisfying periods of my life, and I shall always be grateful for that wonderful opportunity."

Professor Doris Meyer, Sports Sciences, praised her students "who really kept me on my toes. I always felt the responsibility of presenting an outstanding class session, material that was usable, carefully and creatively prepared, and enthusiastically delivered. My students were the best and deserved the best."

Kathleen Shannon writes from her home in Portland, Oregon, "One last afternoon while working in my Sears Hall office, I heard someone running up the stairs—taking three steps at a time. The door burst open and there stood one of my students, a very tall star basketball player. Breathlessly he blurted, 'Miss Shannon, will you go with me to the Basketball Awards Banquet?' I listened in amazement. 'Thank you for the honor,' I replied, 'but you'd take a terrible razzing from your teammates if you showed up with your Religious Studies professor as your guest.' He reassured me, 'Please, I really want you to. My mom and my girlfriend will be going also.' So on that night he called for me, very dressed up, driving a big car. I was warmly greeted and introduced by coaches and administrators, one of whom said, 'I'll bet you're the only faculty member ever invited as a player's guest.' My host won the MVP Award, but what he gave me that night was more than an award."

When Elizabeth L. Spelts retired from the Conservatory of Music she was honored by her colleagues in a tribute to her "50 Years of Singing and Teaching in Stockton, California." Written compliments were extended from Conservatory Dean Carl Nosse, and from Todd Duncan, creator of the role of Porgy in *Porgy and Bess*, Metropolitan Opera singer, and Professor at Philadelphia's Curtis Institute of Music. Colleagues and former students who performed for her at the tribute concert were Seija Anderson, soprano; George Buckbee, pianist; Joan Coulter, pianist; Ira Lehn, cellist; Anastasios Vrenios, tenor; Elizabeth Kirkpatrick Vrenios, soprano; William Whitesides, tenor; and Frank Wiens, pianist.

In the 1960s, Thuan Van Nguyen happened to meet a lieutenant and UOP graduate who told him that "the University of the Pacific is a school where each student is a human being and not a statistic." Van Nguyen was so impressed that he eventually "landed at Pacific as a professor of electrical engineering." He concludes with this comic parting shot, "When I came to the Stockton campus of UOP in 1969, there were one president, two vice presidents, and about 4,500 students. Now, there are one president, one provost, three vice presidents, two assistants to the president, four associate/assistant provosts, and about 4,500 students."

W. C. "Mike" Wagner, Professor of Economics and Social Science, and a premier hire in the Cluster College years, pays tribute to Raymond College as a "precious experience: the gracious gift of the Raymond family, the embrace of the university community, dedicated faculty, and probing students all created an ideal atmosphere for cultivating the life of the mind: it was not only heady, it was bracing and beautiful."

The generosity of students, faculty, and staff shines through in a story told by Roy A. Whiteker, former COP Dean and Professor of Chemistry: "At the 1982 COP Commencement, the Dean challenged the college community to participate in the newly opened Library Campaign. University representatives developed strategies, and Regent Bob Eberhardt matched all campus donations. A Fall Carnival featured Dean Whiteker and ASUOP President Joe Hartley in a dunk tank, buttons proclaimed the wearer as a 'Library Lover,' and the winner of the door prize at the wrap-up party at the Stockton Airport flew off for a weekend in San Francisco. Although there were no salary raises that fall, 177 students and 400 university personnel gave $85,000, of which 150 COP faculty and staff contributed $50,000. To recognize the leadership role of the 'COP Dean and Faculty' the Library named its reference section for them."

No more thoughts need be imparted about compassion, generosity, caring, intellectual challenges, dedication, achievements—all and more are here in these "Remembrances of Things Past."

CHAPTER THREE

THE UNIVERSITY AS CATALYST FOR CHANGE

It is a paradox: while tradition-bound and fixed in ideals and place, the university has become a powerful agent of change.

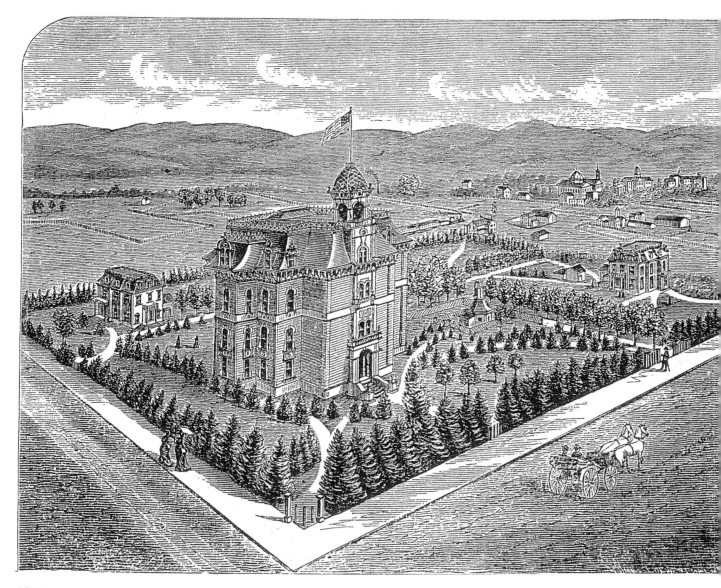

1875

———

"College Park," San Jose campus. Pictured are West Hall and to the rear, administration library, classrooms, and residence hall.

The Way We Were Then...

1923-24

COP sets up shop in Stockton Record *building*

1890s

Conservatory of Music on San Jose campus.

Beginnings of the Stockton campus in 1927. Prominent buildings are Conservatory of Music, Weber Hall, Administration Building (Knoles Hall), North Hall, South Hall, Anderson Hall, Power House, and West Memorial Infirmary.

The discovery of gold in central California in January of 1848 produced vast changes in the west: strangers from all parts of the world, burgeoning business, new towns, and lo!—centers of learning. Methodists out east knew a good thing when they saw one, and that meant dispatching missionaries straightaway.

Driven by enthusiasm to foster the church, by altruism to further causes of good, by zeal to promote education, they advanced to the Golden State by land and by sea. The three ministers arriving first in 1849-50 were eventually to be known as the Founding Fathers of the college-cum-university.

Edward Bannister, one of the missionaries to gold country.

Bearded Dr. Edward Bannister of the Baltimore Conference, who settled into San Jose after sailing around the Horn up to San Francisco, later became the university's first president, pro tem.

Fiery Reverend William Taylor, also of Baltimore and also voyager by sea, stopped and stayed in San Francisco. In future years he gained even greater renown as Bishop of Africa.

And open-faced, rotund Reverend Isaac Owen spent many weeks slogging overland by oxen teams to his appointed work as a church administrator in Sacramento and afterwards in San Jose, where he acquired a reputation as an avid reader and dedicated promulgator of higher education.

This triumvirate, along with eight other important ministers and laymen (Captain Joseph Aram, Martin C. Briggs, who later served as president of Pacific, W. Grove Deal, Craven P. Hester, Annis Merrill, William Morrow, Daniel L. Ross, and S. D. Simonds) pushed the idea of a "seminary of learning" in California under the patronage and control of the Methodist Church.

Among possible sites for the proposed new college were San Francisco, San Jose, Santa Clara, and Vallejo. The Santa Clara site won out with an endowment of $27,500. The first name selected—California Wesleyan College—didn't last long, however, because the Methodist Church already had too many "Wesleyans"; competing Catholic institutions had a deeper reservoir of saint names. So the Founding Fathers then chose a name as grand and challenging as the ocean: University of the Pacific, "a big name to grow up and into," one of the ministers said.

On the 10th of July, 1851, Pacific became the first chartered institution of higher learning in the state of California and certainly ranked among the first few in all the west. After the name change from "College" to "University," it would return again to "College" for a half century, and then finally back to "University" at the beginning of the 1960s.

Pacific's historical mural is remarkably colorful: tough times, bold strides, financial emergencies, hallmarks of faculty scholarship, sprouting of buildings, student disruptions, fires, salary sacrifices, changes of campus location, inspired teaching, fluctuating enrollments, sports heroism, administrative triumphs and debacles, parties and grinds, student scholastic achievements. For all the ups and downs, progress kept resulting.

For instance, the Founding Fathers deserve commendation for their unbiased and forward-looking attitude toward women. As chauvinistic as their church may have been in those early days, it nevertheless pushed hard for female education. Thus in

l853, it set forth a plan for the first "Female Collegiate Institute" in a separate building at Santa Clara. By 1858, five women graduated (as "Mistress of Science"), along with five men. However, not until 1871 and the university's move to San Jose did coeducation become a reality.

Let's pause here to consider some implications of time.

In the history of Europe or Asia, a 150-year period flows as a mere ripple, but for us in the United States—particularly California—it's a long, long time.

The founding of University of the Pacific, the start of the California Gold Rush, the birth of Stockton as a city, and the admission of California as a state all occurred within two-to-three years of one another. Moreover, California underwent a population explosion as it grew by a third of a million in the six years following the discovery of gold: the greatest mass migration in the history of the country. San Francisco's population increased by 60 times in a dozen years.

The university was already celebrating its 50th anniversary the year that Queen Victoria died, its 100th anniversary when nuclear bombs were being tested and the Cold War was heating up, its 150th anniversary after the disputatious election of our 43rd U.S. President. Thus the university has been around through 30 of those presidents, going back to a time when the U.S.A. consisted of only 31 states. At the chartering of the college by the California Supreme Court in the summer of l851, Millard Fillmore held office as our 13th President, a decade before the advent of Abraham Lincoln, our l6th, and the beginning of the American Civil War. Also in 1851 Napoleon III declared the Second Empire in France. The following statistics might cause the parents of current students an amused wince: in the 1850s, college tuition, room and board amounted to $170 per semester; by 1929 tuition had climbed to $6 per unit. Remember, too, that in the 1850s public education was almost unheard of. For lack of public schools, three of every four children went without rudimentary training in the three Rs.

1906
—————

Rubble at East Hall in San Jose, caused by the earthquake in Point Arena.

1909
—————

President W. W. Guth changed the name of the university back to College of the Pacific in 1911.

The university kept up slow growth, but attempts to maintain a medical school proved troublesome. Medical training began in 1859, the Civil War then caused disruptions, and finally in 1873 the medical department melded into the Cooper Medical School in San Francisco, and eventually became the California Pacific Medical Center.

As a pioneering private school, Pacific struggled in the 1860s. An energetic financial agent, Greenberry R. Baker, led a cost-cutting move from Santa Clara to "Stockton Ranch" (later called "College Park") in San Jose. With this transferral in 1871, and the commingling in classes of male and female students, came status among California's first coeducational colleges. An unshared ranking of #1 occurred seven years later with the establishment of the Conservatory of Music, the first associated with a university in California, and, to be even more precise, the first west of Chicago.

The university continued on a fairly even keel through the 1880s and into the '90s, when by a stroke of good planning it managed to consolidate with Napa College, formerly Napa Collegiate Institute, although the loss of the college came as an unsettling blow to the city of Napa.

In the mid '90s, President A. C. Hirst, who had succeeded the prosperous administration of C. C. Stratton, ran into trouble with both students and faculty. Competition between classes instigated by Hirst in pursuit of "collegiate spirit" led to riotous behavior by the class of 1894 (freshmen of 1890). As a result of his arbitrariness and obstinacy, Hirst came off the worse for wear and left abruptly. Later presidents and acting presidents fared scarcely better—average tenures in office lasted only a half decade—but they were men of good will and worked hard to maintain the university. This group includes James N. Beard, Isaac Crook, Moses S. Cross, Eli McClish, and Bert J. Morris. Enjoined to leave the presidency of Napa College for the more demanding position in San Jose, McClish had the honor of presiding at UOP's fiftieth jubilee celebration.

In the time of the great San Francisco Earthquake, during which rattled East Hall lost its top floor, McClish resigned, leading to the inauguration of W. W. Guth in 1909. As if to confirm its status as a small liberal arts college, Guth ordered a name change, so, back it went to College of the Pacific in 1911.

Consider, again, for a moment the pre-move time line: World War I had yet to be fought. America would enter the war in 1917—a considerable number of Pacific students and alumni enlisted for duty. Toward the end of the war, a flu epidemic raged. It also struck Pacific, as did two serious fires in 1914 and 1915 that burned Central Hall and West Hall, both in the first part of John L. Seaton's tenure as president. Even this early on, Pacific made itself known in sports. In 1916, R. S. Wright—acclaimed as the best rugby fullback in the country—represented the college in the All-American-All-British rugby game.

The college sought dramatic change at the selection of Tully Cleon Knoles as its 19th president in 1919. A USC graduate, then-history professor at his alma mater, a colorful orator, skilled arbitrator, expert horseman, Knoles brought flamboyance, enthusiasm, and panache to a position that he was to hold for more than a quarter of a century. He served another dozen years as chancellor, making a total of 40 years that he devoted to Pacific.

In the early 1920s, Knoles and his staff faced a momentous decision. Pinched by

1920s

Tully C. Knoles, 19th president, prided himself on his horsemanship.

the closeness of Stanford and Berkeley, facing the prospect of reduction to a two-year college, they were compelled to move to a new location. The proximity of the Catholic college at Santa Clara and the teachers' college eventually to become San Jose State University, along with lack of room for expansion and the noisy distractions of frequent trains, were among other reasons behind a move. At the same time, COP sought to maintain reasonable medium size. It wanted most of all to retain its admired reputation for more personal relationships between teachers and students. Its advantages had always been smaller classes and closer association of students, faculty, staff, administrators, and supporters. The General Education Board in New York that Knoles consulted, i.e., the Rockefeller Foundation, unequivocally suggested the San Joaquin Valley. Principal sites considered were Modesto, Stockton, Sacramento; lesser possibilities included Lodi, Oakland, and Turlock.

Stockton made a very strong pitch. The J. C. Smith Company offered sizable parcels of land, besides funding for needed buildings. Far-seeing Stocktonians, such as banker G. E. L. Wilhoit, Methodist minister A. C. Bane, Stockton *Record* publisher Irving Martin, along with Trustee Thomas Baxter, and college vice-president John L. Burcham proved formidable proponents in the victory for Stockton. Bane remarked, "I think that Stockton has won the greatest prize of her existence." All agreed on the plot of land—eventually a total of 71 acres—along the south bank of the *Calaveras River* as ideal. So came the third and final move of the college to Stockton in 1924.

Freshmen classes had already begun the preceding year in the *Record* building; teacher training developed under the aegis of a now-professional School of Education; beginning construction officially formalized the move; and the Stockton campus— to cheery huzzahs—was dedicated in 1925. All but two of the faculty in San Jose moved with their families to Stockton, most to a tract called The Manor, or, by some, Egghead Row.

Upon the move, enrollment increased almost immediately, and it became abundantly clear at a 75th anniversary jubilee in mid-June, 1926, that the college had finally found its right home—this time, after much travail, its permanent home. So the third: the lucky charm. But luck rarely happens without hard work. Years of development lay ahead in building up of the campus; always money had to be raised and debt eliminated—no easy task as the the Great Depression approached.

President Knoles led a concerted effort to elevate standards for entering students and to reduce the ratio of enrollees to degrees, which is to say that Pacific's faculty and courses became so appealing that more and more students stayed through graduation. In 1927 a long-established ban on dancing was lifted—to the jubilation of students waiting to cut loose on the Charleston. And then came the Crash that resulted in nationwide financial crises and joblessness.

1940s
_____

V-12 trainees at COP during World War II.

By now, Pacific had passed its 80th year; Franklin D. Roosevelt would hold the office of U. S. President for the next 13 years; forces of fascism and militarism rose in Europe and Japan; the dual anathema of Holocaust and World War II awaited.

For Tully Knoles and his intrepid colleagues, the problems of the Thirties needed local solutions. Faculty and administrators took voluntary salary cuts; tuition payments changed, and, most importantly, sweeping curricular changes were initiated, all as a means to fight off the debilitating Depression. That third solution involved substantive changes in which the entire structure of the college underwent alteration. Course offerings were limited to junior, senior, and graduate students in the college, while lower division work went on at Stockton College, a public institution run by the Stockton School District. Interestingly, college facilities served for both. This extraordinary mix of private and public higher education, which had been approved by a unique vote of the State Supreme Court, lasted from 1936 to 1951.

As with the earlier Depression, the college managed tenaciously to survive diminished enrollments and financial stress during World War II. COP's successful operation of Naval and Marine V-12 programs helped to keep the college afloat; its enduring appeal brought back from the war many veterans who had begun their military-college training in Stockton. In 1948-49, the college enrolled more than 600 veterans under the GI Bill. In this period, too, COP's Tigers recorded impressive winning seasons in football. The famed 1949 team, coached by Larry Siemering and quarterbacked by Eddie LeBaron, remained unbeaten and untied through twelve games, amassing 575 points to its opponents 66. In its 99th year (the 93rd Commencement, of 1950), the college awarded more than 400 bachelor's degrees, three dozen M.A.'s, and more than 200 teaching credentials. Pacific had arrived.

After the inauguration in 1947 of President Burns, the college took yet greater strides in growth. Burns's chief aides in this period were Vice President Burcham and Ted Baun, president of the trustees. Consider this progress at mid-century:

1949

One of the best teams in the nation: unbeaten, untied, and uninvited to any bowl game.

- Fifteen new buildings constructed.
- Barracks like Bannister Hall and Owen Hall put into use.
- The dedication of Pacific Memorial Stadium in 1950.
- Marked improvement in facilities for the sciences, humanities, social sciences.
- Double- and triple-fold enrollments in the late Forties and into the Fifties.
- Founding of the Pacific Marine Biology research station in 1948 at Dillon Beach.
- Setting up of the California History Foundation with Emeritus USC Professor Rockwell D. Hunt in charge.
- Championing of academic freedom by sponsorship of controversial speakers and panel discussions.

In the Fifties and Sixties, development and building of the School of Pharmacy began on acquired land north of the Calaveras. By hiring away Dean Ivan Rowland from Idaho State, adding new faculty, and initiating a demanding multifaceted pharmacy program, the college answered a definite need for well trained pharmacists along the Pacific Coast and inland.

In 1956 the Graduate School formed (although a first graduate degree had been granted as far back as 1861), and two years later the School of Engineering was established. Praiseworthy accomplishments by each school were to follow.

The School of Pharmacy makes great strides forward in the 1950s. Its pharmacy center was completed in 1969.

And, here, another remarkable testament to faculty loyalty: a quarter century after having made the move from San Jose, eleven professors were still at the Stockton campus: Allan Bacon, J. Russell Bodley, DeMarcus Brown, George H. Colliver, Fred L. Farley, J. William Harris, H. J. Jonte, Lorraine Knoles, Monreo Potts, G. A. Werner, G. Warren White. They call to mind the loyalty of such later staff members as Pearl Piper, who started at Pacific in 1940, worked steadily for 46 years, and is still serving on a part-time basis at the John Muir Center; and Jim Bratcher of Duplicating Services, who retired recently after more than four decades with the university.

President Robert E. Burns and the Memorial Tower named after him. The building, which contains a large water tank behind its stained-glass windows, was dedicated in 1964.

As the college prepared to enter the 1960s, Burns and his staff saw the necessity to expand, but not in traditional ways. In his inaugural address a dozen years before, Burns had cited the need for a dynamic community of scholars to "Pioneer or Perish." (The phrase serves as the title, appropriately, of an excellent book about the Burns administration by Kara Pratt Brewer, 1st ed., 1977, reprinted, 1998.) Burns's idea to establish cluster colleges along the lines of Oxford and Cambridge—as he put it, "the Oxbridge Way"—would represent, he thought, a change from the large impersonal state institutions. Vision became reality, carried out with swiftness and aplomb. Raymond College, stressing liberal arts and small tutorials, formed in 1961 at the generous bequest of Mr. and Mrs. Walter B. Raymond. Then in 1963 came Elbert Covell College, a bilingual, bicultural college emphasizing English-speaking for Latin American students and Spanish-speaking for their North American counterparts, at the generous bequest of Elbert Covell; and, last, Callison College, with its focus upon international studies, during which students spent a full year in India or Japan. Generous benefactors Dr. and Mrs. Ferd Callison were responsible for funding that college. Each of the cluster colleges had its own faculty and its own curriculum. The cluster college plan fared well for a time and produced many fine graduates, but eventually the colleges were absorbed back into the traditional university curriculum.

And, speaking of "university," the time had come—1961—for a change of name back to "University of the Pacific." Also, the Burnsian notion of a tightly knit "Pacific Family" diminished some with changes to a more secularized, a more specialized, a more cosmopolitan university, yet the phrase remains *au courant* because of its recurring emphasis on relationships.

Another major development in the life of the university occurred in the early Sixties with the acquisition of the Dental School from the old College of Physicians and Surgeons in San Francisco. The transfer took place in 1962, and by 1967 the Dental School had moved into an impressive new building at 2155 Webster Street, which it occupies today. The school flourishes under the preeminent leadership of Dr. Arthur Dugoni, a former president of the American Dental Association, serving in his 23rd year as Dean. Enhanced by its much-praised humanistic approach to education ("We build people and along the way they become doctors"), the School of Dentistry grew over a generation from little-known status to world-renown. From 1974 on, dentists-to-be benefited from the school's innovative, streamlined curriculum in which a four-year academic program is completed in three calendar years. The School of

Dentistry is now recognized for its state-of-the-art facilities, its admired outreach clinical programs for comprehensive patient care, its outstanding faculty, and, most importantly, its highly skilled graduates, who, while pursuing their professional careers, tend also to become caring, involved community leaders.

This addition fulfilled the second part of UOP's modern tripartite campus in Stockton-San Francisco-Sacramento.

The third was completed in 1966 when McGeorge School of Law merged into the University of the Pacific. Originally established in 1924 by Verne McGeorge, a Sacramento attorney, and named for him at his death in 1929, the law school sprang from small beginnings, moving from downtown Sacramento to the Oak Park area in 1957 and gaining ABA accreditation in 1966. Dean Gordon Schaber worked closely with President Burns and others to expand and develop its programs and facilities. Now consisting of two dozen buildings on an ideal 21-acre campus, McGeorge School of Law offers full-time Day and part-time Evening Divisions. Internationally known for the excellence of its faculty and the successes of its graduates, McGeorge, led by Dean Gerald Caplan, is considered one of the premier law schools in the west.

If an operative word applies over 77 years of UOP in Stockton, it is CHANGE. Always change. Pacific has always been flexible, always willing to try new methods, always willing to adapt as educational needs arise.

Case in point. While intangible, a major change occurred in the university's relationship with the Methodist Church. Ties to the church remained long and honorable for 118 years. In 1969 the university's Board of Regents and the California-Nevada Annual Conference of the United Methodist Church discontinued their formal legal relationship. While UOP remains among 122 national and 340 world-wide United Methodist-related schools, colleges, and universities, it has become an independent entity, with its own appointed Board of Regents. Despite its now less-than-direct religious affiliation, the university takes pride in its long linking with the United Methodist Church. Appropriately, Stockton's Central Methodist Church sits directly across Pacific Avenue from the main campus and the university's nondenominational Morris Chapel, as if a constant reminder of the old bond.

On the other hand, tangible changes on campus in the Sixties were evident in the number of new faculty hires and in new buildings springing up, especially the Robert E. Burns Memorial Tower, dedicated in 1964. Department heads under Dean Harold Jacoby at COP, as well as deans of the

The stunning stained-glass windows of Morris Chapel, completed and dedicated in 1942.

Students and faculty protest the Cambodian Incursion during the Vietnam War.

professional schools, sought out the best young Ph.D.s that could be found around the country. Most taught into the 1990s; some are still around at the turn of the century. They continue the long tradition of first-rate teachers from early days, like Professor James N. Martin of Ancient Languages in the 1870s and 1880s; Etta E. Booth, Fine Arts, who served for decades at Napa College, San Jose, and Stockton; mid-20th century historians like R. Coke Wood, Malcolm Eiselen, Malcolm Moule; modern sociologists such as Fay Goleman and George Lewis; a contemporary artist like Gil Dellinger, or a scientist like Carl Wulfman. For others, see tributes by former students to professors who profoundly influenced them and also consult lists of Spanos Distinguished Teaching Awards for COP, and University Distinguished Faculty Awards.

Meantime, students were adjusting to the tumultuous 1960s. While rambunctious and independent, Pacific students were never violently radicalized. They demonstrated, marched, protested, but their behavior did not disintegrate into riot and chaos. By the mid-'70s, the Vietnam War had finally come to its painful end, and campus life returned to less volatile pursuits.

Sadly, the two figures who had dominated Pacific's administrative life for more than fifty years had by now died: Tully Knoles in 1959 at the age of 83, and Robert E. Burns in 1971 at the early age of 61.

Changes continued over the next three decades in the capable hands of three more presidents. From 1851 to 1919, sixty-some years, the college/university had 18 presidents; in the 82 years since, only five. Obviously the result has been far greater stability and consistency. Starting 77 years ago, with the move to Stockton, the presidents have been, besides Knoles to 1946 and Burns to 1971, Stanley E. McCaffrey, from 1971 to 1987; Bill L. Atchley, from 1987 to 1995; and Donald V. DeRosa, from 1995 into the new millennium, the university's current president.

Stanley E. McCaffrey, President of Pacific from 1971 to 1987.

McCaffrey and his staff added substantially to the physical improvement of the Stockton campus, its professional schools, and both the law school and dental school. In 1972 University College was established for reentry students, especially older adults wanting to resume their education after prolonged delay; and construction started on the McGeorge School of Law "Courtroom of the Future," an event which received national attention.

1974 became a landmark year for Pacific in terms of expansion. The most overt physical change to occur on the Stockton campus resulted from the purchase of the former Delta College grounds (now UOP's South Campus). Within a few years, some thirty buildings were removed, the new Science Center installed, the Long Theatre renovated, and the School of Education moved from Owen Hall to the old Delta Library building.

Thus the South Campus was becoming integrated into a new fully developed three-part campus: North (i.e., north of the Calaveras), Central (north of Stadium Drive, to the river), and South (south of Stadium Drive to Mendocino). Further unification of these campuses will continue into the next decade. A major change in the South Campus, for instance, has occurred just at the millennium with the completion of the impressive new Arts and Geosciences Center, thanks to major support from Jeanette and Robert Powell of Sacramento. Further refinements also continue, of course, at the professional schools of Law in Sacramento and Dentistry in San Francisco.

Never content to rest on its laurels, the university worked constantly to fine tune its academic programs. During the late 1960s and into the 1970s, wholesale curriculum revision of liberal arts, supported by a Danforth Foundation study, resulted in sweeping changes in course offerings and scheduling. As a related innovation, Winter Term—in which students concentrated on one four-unit course in January—went into effect in 1970 and lasted for a dozen years. Similarly, an I & I (Information and Imagination) program evolved out of cooperation among different academic disciplines to form a new general education plan for freshmen—it has since been replaced by Mentor Seminars, fostered by COP Dean Robert Benedetti, for both freshman and senior years. The university also initiated CIP, a Community Involvement Program, in which 200 disadvantaged Stockton students who could qualify academically were allowed to matriculate on a scholarship basis. The program, now 30 years old, has produced two thousand noteworthy graduates, all of whom performed lengthy community service during and after their studies. Some 85 percent of CIP graduates continue to reside in Stockton and its environs.

With expansion and growth also came reduction and integration. The Marine Station at Dillon Beach had long since closed. In the late 1970s-early 1980s, combined forces from the cluster colleges and COP worked toward establishing an international program until finally in 1986 a suitable consolidation resulted, with the founding of the School of International Studies, offering a challenging array of undergraduate courses devoted to global issues, and to historical, economic, and cultural relations. This demanding interdisciplinary work also combines with required study abroad.

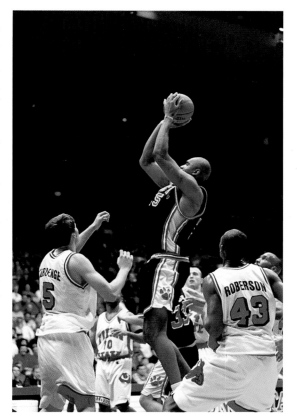

Pacific graduate Michael Olowakandi '98, now an NBA player.

Meantime the university opened its Spanos Center—a multipurpose complex for sports like basketball, volleyball, wrestling, and for concerts, conferences, and other community events, with seating ranging from 6,000 to 10,000. The center is named for its principal benefactor: Alex G. Spanos, a COP alumnus who rose from modest beginnings in Stockton, and went on to become a builder/developer of national reputation, and a respected owner within the National Football League.

Rabid crowds have cheered on any number of the university's stellar teams there. When women's volleyball began in 1975, no one would have dreamed that the Lady Tigers would win back-to-back national championships in 1985 and 1986, maintain consistent national ranking every year, and in 1999 reach the semifinals, losing to eventual champion Penn State in a fiercely contested five-game thriller. Similarly, when the son of a Nigerian diplomat telephoned from London to inquire about basketball at Pacific, no one dreamed that Michael Olowokandi would become a world-famous walk-on and the #1 player taken in 1998's NBA Draft.

Change and betterment—the bywords kept on. In 1982 a campaign began to dou-

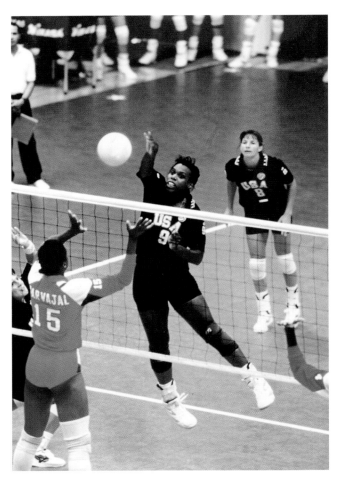

Elaina Oden '90, champion Pacific volleyballer, went on to represent the U.S.A. at the 1992 and '96 Olympics.

ble the size of the library; by 1986 the William Knox Holt Library was dedicated, and by 1999 students were benefiting from use of an expansive new library computer center, with multiple terminals. In 1984 Weber Hall underwent renovation for the School of Business and Public Administration, later renamed for benefactor Robert M. Eberhardt and the Eberhardt family, many of whom are alumni. Business added a Master's program in 1992. Innovative programs in constantly expanding fields of business, government, public organizations, entrepreneurship, among others, are taught by experts able to back their knowledge with practical, hands-on experience.

Before the changing of the guard to Atchley's watch, McCaffrey helped peripherally to put Pacific in the limelight while serving as President of Rotary International during a year's leave. This honor also befell Executive Vice-President Clifford Dochterman two years later—an extraordinary achievement to have two International Rotary Presidents from the same city and the same university.

Continued improvement in the physical plenitude of the university's campuses marked Bill Atchley's eight-year term. He succeeded to a considerable extent in bettering Pacific's financial position, particularly in increasing endowment funds and reducing sizable debts. In 1988, *U. S. News and World Report* ranked UOP in the top 125 universities and colleges, and 22nd among comprehensive institutions which offered a broad range of liberal arts, science courses, and professional programs. Major developments continue to unfold in health and science programs, for example, in such fields as speech-language pathology, sports medicine, and physical therapy.

Anyone with university allegiance loves new buildings. There they stand as signs of fulfillment, progress, commitment. Pacific has had no lack of them in the last couple of decades: the McCaffrey Center and Student Union; two rehearsal halls, a classroom building; a refurbished auditorium, renamed the Faye Spanos Concert Hall. Its dedication in 1986 drew such celebrities as Bob Hope, Diahann Carroll, Vic Damone, and Telly Savalas. Add the Khoury Engineering building; Baun Fitness Center; new aquatics, softball, and tennis facilities; modernized plant operations; and renovated residence halls. Nor has the university slighted facilities for research and scholarship. Mention should also be made of the Holt-Atherton Special Collections, with its prized John Muir Papers and the new Dave and Iola Brubeck Collection.

As Pacific moved into the 1990s its home state and the world were undergoing troublesome problems with economy, labor, housing, population. There could no longer be business as usual in the academy, given the necessity for sound institutional planning, participatory governance, accountability. An upturn was about to begin.

Following the late Robert M. Eberhardt, then Dale Reddig, as chair of the Board of Regents, successor Robert T. Monagan became the right man at the right time, possessing experience and skills. He led the search for a new president after the resignation of Atchley. On February 22, 1995, the Regents appointed Donald DeRosa as the university's 23rd president and only the fifth since the campus relocation to Stockton in 1924. Young and energetic, a former provost at the University of North Carolina at Greensboro, DeRosa saw his challenge as fulfilling for Pacific "the vision for academic distinctiveness that Robert Burns had set three decades earlier."

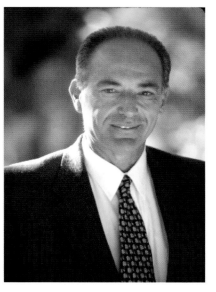

Donald V. DeRosa, current president of Pacific, appointed February 22, 1995.

Such an undertaking required a series of tough decisions, including the eventual suspension of intercollegiate football, necessitated by Pacific's short-term financial plight and other exigencies. He also recognized that academic programs, which had grown more by accretion than by designed planning, needed attention by the faculty. To help lead reviews of programs and finances, DeRosa set out immediately to build a leadership team. He recruited Philip N. Gilbertson as Provost and Patrick Cavanaugh as vice president for business and finance to assist him and the faculty in a top-to-bottom review of academic, administrative, and governance practices. Contributing four decades of experience and expertise to this new team was Judith Chambers, Vice President for Student Life. Besides her numerous administrative tasks and personal contacts with many individual students, she oversees more than one hundred student organizations.

Among first items of business for faculty and the new administration were development of a statement describing Pacific's mission, the vision for fulfilling it, and a set of priorities to guide the annual budget process. Adopted by the Board of Regents in 1996, the university's mission "is to provide a superior, student-centered learning environment integrating liberal arts and professional education and preparing individuals for lasting achievement and responsible leadership in their careers and communities."

A vision statement, endorsed by Regents in 1997, calls for the university to be "nationally known for linking liberal arts and professional education through innovative curricular and co-curricular programs of exceptional quality and high value. The university will strengthen its visibility and take full advantage of the rich resources of Northern California. Pacific will become a national leader in the creative use of internships and leadership development programs. These distinctive features will be shaped by our commitment to equip Pacific graduates for success in a multi-cultural and international society."

Next came review of academic curricula, which led to reevaluation of program offerings, cutting of some underenrolled classes and borderline majors, reduction of general degree programs. Planning assumptions and priorities are subject to further analysis and redefinition. A few of the initiatives include experiential learning, increased student retention, faculty and alumni participation, strengthening ties with alumni, information technology, community partnerships, and teacher-scholar models. Outstanding teaching always remains a principal goal with a high ratio of full-time faculty teaching classes from freshmen to senior and graduate levels, as Pacific seeks to avoid the reliance on part-time faculty and graduate assistants that is plaguing so many modern-day colleges and universities.

By the late Nineties, Pacific, like the state of California, had turned a corner toward a better future. As a result of belt-tightening measures, UOP's financial position improved markedly. First a major bank debt was diminished; then long-time Pacific supporter Gladys L. Benerd established an $11 million trust for the School of Education, now named in her memory and for the library; enrollment for entering freshmen increased to capacity on the Stockton campus; the quality of those students steadily improved; physical facilities were constantly upgraded; and, finally, school endowment reached a new high of $116 million. Plans to triple the university's endowment are underway. As an example of a healthy division, the School of Dentistry in San Francisco has five endowed professorships, two endowed chairs, and $39 million in realized and expected endowments. The goal, under President DeRosa's productive guidance, is to keep striving for academic distinction. Current accrediting by WASC has proven these tactical successes because the university received the maximum ten-year accreditation, including special commendation for the strength of student-faculty interaction. Similarly the Commission on Dental Accreditation bestowed upon the School of Dentistry 18 commendations.

Olympian Bradley Schumacher '97, swimming and water polo star.

At crucial times in the past, Pacific has taken bold steps to assure its continued success. The move to Stockton, survival tactics during the Depression, the addition of professional schools and cluster colleges in the postwar period serve as examples. As the Sesquicentennial neared, President DeRosa called on more than 250 alumni and friends to undertake a pioneering effort that will create the most flourishing prospects for Pacific. His "Commission on the Next Level of Excellence" consists of seven panels evaluating the complete range of University operations. When work is completed, the President will recommend to the Regents areas of greatest promise for reaching yet higher levels of distinctiveness. This ambitious program challenges the University community, as never before, to create a bright future for Pacific.

As for other strengths, Pacific's ambiance is perfectly made for intellectual and cultural events: music camps, dance festivals, art exhibits; the Pacific Rim Conference, the first of its kind in 1994; packed houses during two decades for appearances by such writers and poets as Larry McMurtry, Isabel Allende, Tony Hillerman, Nikki Giovanni, Peter Matthiessen, Ray Bradbury, Robert Pinsky, and Frances Mayes, the first in 2000, at the Marion Jacobs Literary Forum.

The San Francisco 49ers chose UOP's Stockton campus as the team's official summer training camp. The 49ers' presence has been hugely beneficial to the university, the entire Stockton community, and loyal out-of-town fans. The training camp arrangement helped somewhat to assuage disappointment at news to boosters that the university was dropping its well-storied collegiate football program. The suspension, underway now for five years, will be periodically re-examined. Meanwhile sports shine on for Tiger fans. In the 1996 summer Olympic Games in Atlanta, Pacific's Bradley Schumacher won two gold medals in swimming, and competed in water polo in the 2000 Games in Sydney, Australia. In both 1999 and 2000 Pacific won the Big West Conference Commissioner's Cup, presented for the best overall results among 12 universities in 18 annual conference championships. The men's and women's sports include baseball, basketball, softball, soccer, swimming, tennis, water polo, and volleyball.

For all its multiplicity, the university remains devoted to inquiry, devoted to transmitting the results of research and interpretation; devoted to teaching and learning; devoted, in sum, to the pursuit of wisdom. Important figures like former president Atchley, veteran COP Dean Harold "Jake" Jacoby, drama director DeMarcus Brown, long-time Regent Ted Baun, and chemistry professor Michael Minch—all lost to death in the turning of 2000—would have agreed in unison that there could be no better calling. And they would have approved the continuing expansion of new offerings and facilities, such as a Pacific Humanities Center and Italian Cultural Center, new clinical facilities for pharmacy and health sciences, a new university center, and the resettling of varied departments as the next decade progresses. Also, in anticipation of enrollment growth on the Stockton campus, groundbreaking took place in October, 2000, on a new $10-million residential apartment community north of the river. The first student residence to be added in the past 22 years, it will house some 200 students

More detailed credit needs to be given to all divisions of the university: its schools of Business, Education, Engineering, International Studies, Music, Pharmacy, its College of the Pacific, University College (for adult re-entry), and Graduate School, its School of Dentistry and School of Law, not to mention superlative support from registrar and libraries, from financial aid and career planning and health services, et al. Limitations of space prevent similar full credit to the former cluster colleges: Raymond, Covell, and Callison. The same holds for community-university interaction and the work of alumni associations.

A century and a half have led to a university firmly established in perfect locations, in excellent health, with an enrollment of nearly 6,000 at its three campuses, looking to its past with pleasure, having produced some 64,000 students. The Stockton campus takes pride in its 39,000 graduates, along with about 6,500 non-grad alumni. Then add nearly 7,000 Dental School graduates and more than 11,000 recipients of J.D. and LL.M. degrees at McGeorge School of Law. Small wonder that the three campuses look to the future with anticipation of the next generations of students and the challenges they present.

As major events occurred in a two-year period around UOP's founding (1851), so have major celebrations occurred in this most recent two-year period. In 1999, Founders Day celebrated the university's 75th year in Stockton, and 2001 marks the Sesquicentennial of its birth, from tiny, tentative beginnings to established accomplishments and acclaim. All this means even greater hopes for the future. The bywords now: bring on the Bicentennial!

Dan Reichert '98, Pacific ace, now pitching for the Kansas City Royals.

The Way We Are Now...

In late summer sunlight and shadows and admidst the redwoods and the sycamores, photographs capture the ivy-and-brick Pacific campus in Stockton as it is today, 77 years after the great relocation from San Jose and 150 years after the State Supreme Court issued the first charter for a California institution of "higher learning."

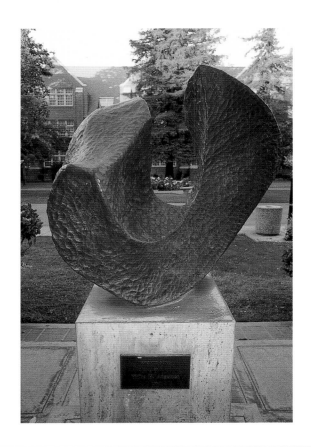

The Way We Will Be...

Students preparing to change the world

Through images of students at practice, study and play, we search for clues that may reveal the way we will be. And as we do, we marvel at the paradox of Pacific: so fixed and unchanging in its traditions and values, yet so transforming in its effects on generation after generation of students.

Pharmacy students Mahinder Virk '02 and Theresa Halperin '02

hether among students or staff, faculty or administrators, personalities flourish at Pacific, and will continue to in the future.

From among countless examples, consider merely these ten Pacific personalities in a slice of time from the early Thirties to the beginning of World War II. As a famed coach forced to retire from Chicago at age 70, Amos Alonzo Stagg came to Pacific's welcoming arms in 1933. His tenure marked Pacific's rise to leadership in intercollegiate athletics and his football teams won national acclaim during his 14 years as coach. A former student body president, Robert E. Burns, ('31) worked as a college fund-raiser while he was courting a pretty student named Grace Weeks—they married in 1934 and later adopted two children who would also graduate from Pacific. Meantime, President Knoles and his wife Emily were parenting eight children, all of whom were to become teachers. Could three students of that decade have predicted in any way what would happen to them? Josephine Kay Van Fleet of Oakland, who took theatre instruction from DeMarcus Brown, went on to win an academy award as Best Supporting Actress in 1955 for her performance in *East of Eden*. Shedding a graduation robe in 1937, Stocktonian John B. Cechini would exchange it years later for the robe of a Superior Court judge. Another young Californian making his way from class to class in the late Thirties and early Forties, Robert T. Monagan, who was a student body leader and talented athlete, became a prominent state politician and currently serves as chair of the university's board of regents. Accomplished comptroller Ovid H. Ritter, while struggling valiantly to keep the college financially solvent, took an interest in campus landscaping and wrote an exegesis of the stained glass windows in Morris Chapel, the cornerstone of which was placed a week after the attack on Pearl Harbor.

It can be expected that well along in the 21st century, similar kinds of stories will emerge about Pacific personalities of this most recent decade.

Conservatory of Music students Jessica Ford '01 and Teresa Woo '01

Nicole Takehara '03

Here they come...

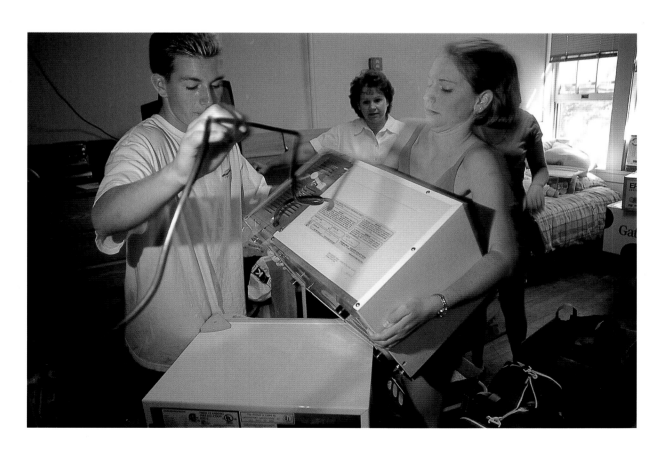

Voice Professor Lynelle Wiens, accompanist Crystal Bloom and Keri Klayko '03

Dave Brubeck, '42, and The Dave Brubeck Quartet, Sesquicentennial Concert, February 3, 2001, Faye Spanos Concert Hall

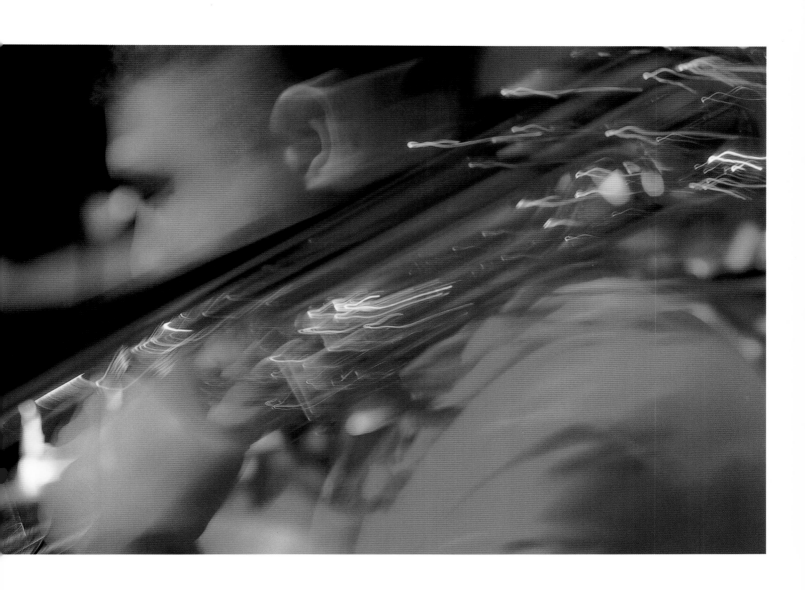

Law Professor David Miller (right) looks over work with Paul Miller, McGeorge '01.

Joanna Roberts, McGeorge '01

Members of Omega Phi Alpha are 'in synch' in the Lip Synch contest.

Kappa Alpha Theta members Kim Burbank (left) '02, Liz Green '02, Meg Wynstra '01 and Nicole Hyde '01 have fun at Fall Festival

Section H saxophonist Keith Kelly

Tony Edwards, Conservatory '97

Professor Jay Leach (right) listens as students present in McGeorge's Courtroom of the Future.

McGeorge Professor Phil Wile

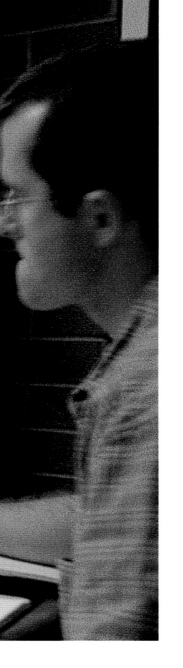

Trial Advocacy Judge Hon. Richard Gilmour

Dr. Keith Ryan, Pediatric Dentistry

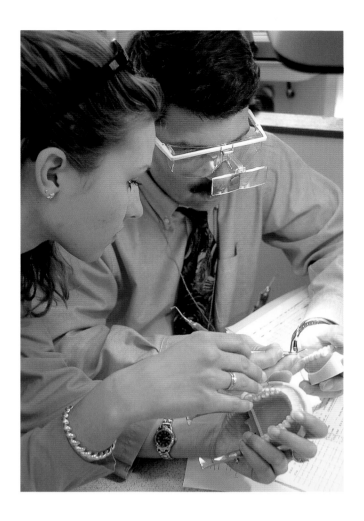

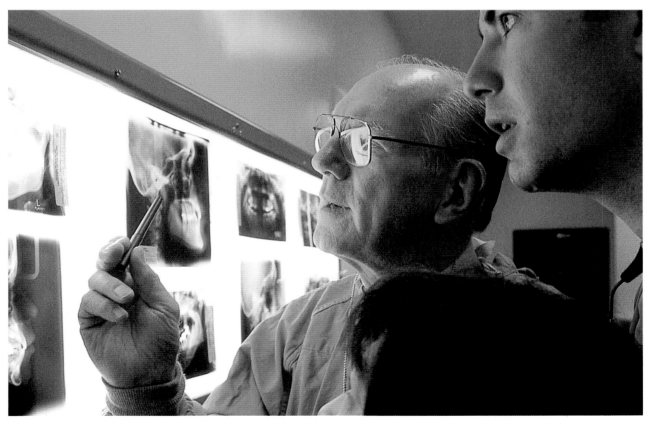

Dr. Jack Hadley, professor and director of emergency services, examines extra-oral radiographs.

Hutto-Patterson Pediatric Clinic

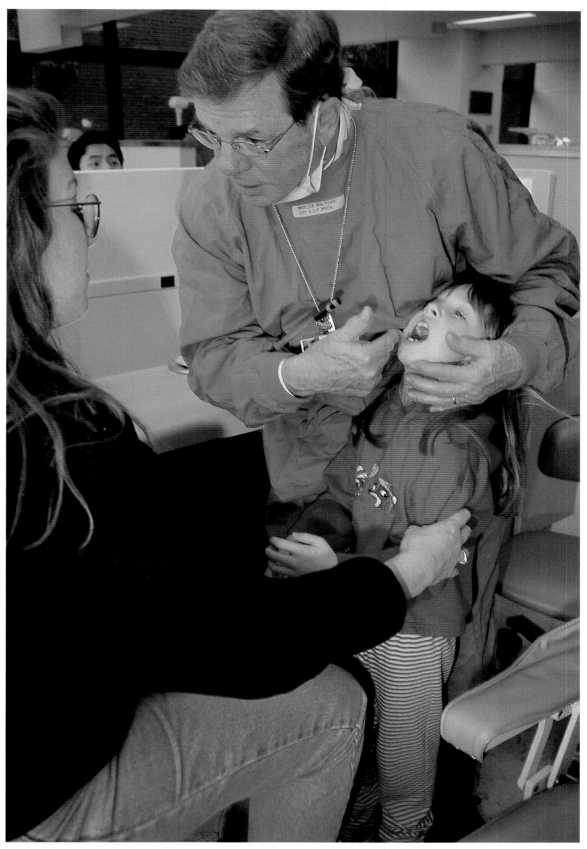

Dr. Ryan counsels Mom on dental care, Hutto-Patterson Pediatric Clinic.

Midnight Madness for Tiger basketball.

Bill Walton '00

Maggie Vineyard (center) '00 and her Delta Gamma sisters enjoy the Madness.

Gabe Esposto '01

Consultation: Pat Donlin (standing right, 5), Brian Basye (6), Daniel Satchkov (2), Chris Nowak (22), Gabe Esposto (in the water right, 13), Kraig Jorgenson (21), Kelly Foot (12), Aaron Silverman (10) and Chris Spencer (7).

No. 5 Pat Donlin with the ball.

Becky Moffitt

Soccer '99: Monica Pires (front right), Becky Moffitt, Carla Burger, Kendra Aston; Jenny Amaya (top right), Angela Allgaier, Christine Bill.

Cindy Ball

Wistrom '00

...And some day they will come home again.

CHAPTER FOUR

Origins

A source guide to the names of Pacific's buildings, residence halls, pathways, landmarks on the Stockton campus

North (of the Calaveras):

Cowell Health Center:	for the S. J. Cowell foundation of San Francisco
Nelson Tennis Courts:	for Harold "Hal" Nelson, late Stockton businessman
Wood Bridge:	for Donald B. Wood, Lodi resident and former regent

Central (between the Calaveras and Stadium Drive/Alpine):

Burns Tower:	for Robert E. Burns, Pacific alumnus and university president from 1946 to l971
Brandenburger Welcome Center, lobby, Burns Tower:	for Roy L. Brandenburger, former regent, of Portola Valley
Morris Chapel:	for donors Percy F. and Lillie B. Morris of Palo Alto
Sears Hall:	in memory of Mr. and Mrs. Joseph Sears by Mr. and Mrs. Osro Sears, benefactors
Colliver Hall:	for Professor George Colliver, a noted Old and New Testament historian, who taught from 1920 to 1957. The Colliver Lectures are named for him.
Harriet M. Smith Memorial Gate at Pacific and Stadium Drive:	by J. C. Smith, who donated an original 40 acres of the campus, in honor of his mother
Faye Spanos Concert Hall at Conservatory of Music:	benefactor, Stockton resident, wife of Alex G. Spanos, matriarch of Spanos family
Dave Brubeck Institute:	for jazz pianist, composer, internationally known musician who attended Pacific
Buck Hall:	for Frank H. Buck of Piedmont, by his widow Eva Buck
McConchie Hall:	for John D. and Mariette McConchie from their daughter Fannie M. McClanahan
Weber Hall:	for Charles M. Weber, founder of Stockton
Eberhardt School of Business:	for Robert M. Eberhardt ('51), long-time benefactor and regent, President of the Bank of Stockton, and for the Eberhardt family
Grace Covell Hall:	for donor and former regent Grace A. Covell
Knoles Hall (and Knoles Lawn):	for Tully C. Knoles, university president from 1919 to 1946; chancellor, 1946-1959
Burcham Walkway:	for John L. Burcham, college vice president
William Knox Holt Memorial Library:	for William Knox Holt, by the Holt family of Stockton
Holt Atherton Conference Room:	from the Stockton-born son of Warren Atherton, who was a noted attorney, American Legion President, and promoter of the GI Bill
Irving Martin Library:	for Irving Martin, Stockton *Record* publisher and Pacific supporter
Atchley Way:	for Bill L. Atchley, UOP's 22nd president, serving from 1987 to 1995
Taylor Conference Room:	for Elliott Taylor, Pacific alumnus, director of counseling, long-time Dean of Admissions
Hand Hall (Hand Hall Lawn):	for Clifford C. Hand, former English professor, COP Dean, and academic vice-president
McCaffrey Center (and McCaffrey Grove):	for Stanley E. McCaffrey, university president from 1971 to 1987
Baun Hall:	for Ted F. Baun, Pacific alumnus in engineering, long-time regent, and university benefactor
Anderson Hall (and Anderson Lawn):	for donors Mr. and Mrs. W. C. Anderson, local farming family
Reynolds Art Gallery:	for Richard Reynolds, artist and Pacific art professor

Khoury Hall:	for Mr. and Mrs. Said Khoury of Kuwait. Their son Toufic graduated from Pacific's School of Engineering in 1980. Many other donors contributed to the building
West Memorial Hall (Finance Center):	for George and Ellen West, and Frank Allen West, by Mrs. Charles M. Jackson in honor of her parents and brother
Ted Baun Student Fitness Center:	see Baun Hall
Stagg Way:	see Stagg Stadium
Bannister Hall:	for Edward Bannister, Methodist minister, founder, first university president; brick facing, a gift from Mrs. Elizabeth Congden
Raney Recreation Area:	after Mrs. Gene (Winifred Olson) Raney of Turlock, a long-time regent
Olson Language Lab:	from Winifred Olson Raney and the Olson family
Owen Hall:	in honor of Isaac Owen, Methodist minister, founder
Wendell Phillips Center:	for the benefactor who was a businessman, explorer, archeologist, oil entrepreneur
Albright Lecture Hall:	for William F. Albright, Biblical archeologist and friend of Wendell Phillips
Muir Center for Regional Studies:	for John Muir, world-famous naturalist, environmentalist, writer
John Ballantyne Hall and Jesse Ballantyne Hall:	for Jesse L. Ballantyne and John N. Ballantyne, farmers and orchardists of Acampo
Bechtel International Center:	from Mr. and Mrs. Stephen D. Bechtel, Sr., and their daughter and son-in-law Mr. and Mrs. Paul L. Davies Jr.
Wilson Hall (formerly the El Centro building):	for George Wilson, long-time regent from Clarksburg
Casa Jackson:	for George and Josephine Jackson by their son, Lester Ramon Jackson of San Francisco
Casa Werner:	for Gustavus A. Werner, an ordained minister and veteran history professor
Baxter Way:	for Thomas F. Baxter, Stockton businessman who helped bring COP to Stockton in 1924. He was president of Holt Manufacturing Company
Carter House:	for Mr. and Mrs. Robert Carter, supporters of Pacific, an Acampo farming family
Raymond Great Hall:	for Mr. and Mrs. Walter B. and Kate Raymond, benefactors of Raymond College, the first of Pacific's cluster colleges
Elbert Covell Dining Hall:	Woodbridge grape grower and vintner, donor of Elbert Covell College, and long-time university benefactor
Eiselen House:	for Malcolm Eiselen, history professor who taught at Pacific from 1927 to 1965
Ritter House:	for Ovid H. Ritter, long-time university administrator and comptroller, by Miss Lucy Ritter, a former regent
Wemyss House:	for Edwin Wemyss, Stockton businessman and benefactor
Farley House:	for Fred Farley, professor of ancient languages and literature and popular liberal arts college dean, who spent 37 years at Pacific
Price House:	for Chalmers G. Price, a Placerville businessman, and Ada Parrish Price
Rudkin Way:	for Jesse Rudkin, a Methodist minister, assistant to President Burns, and director of Development
Bill Simoni Field:	from the Stockton Hall-of-Famer in fast pitching, now a resident of Woodbridge
Amos Alonzo Stagg Memorial Stadium:	A. A. Stagg coached football at Pacific from his 70th to his 84th year. He came to Pacific from Chicago after 41 years of coaching there. He died at age 102 in Stockton in 1965.
Kjeldsen Pool:	for Chris Kjeldsen, swimming coach

South (of Stadium Drive/Alpine):

G. Warren White Entrance
(at Pershing and Alpine):
for a mathematics professor who taught at Pacific for 44 years; also for his wife, Ruby Zahn White

(adjoining) Larry Heller Drive:
for a Pacific football supporter of many years

Zuckerman Field:
sod and improvements by Ed Zuckerman for the entire Zuckerman family, long-time Delta farmers and sod developers

Spanos Center:
for Alex G. Spanos, Pacific alumnus, nationally known developer and philanthropist, owner of the NFL's San Diego Chargers. Mr. Spanos also provided latest new flooring for the center

Anselmo Head-Start Center:
for Sandra "Sandy" Anselmo, respected faculty member in Education, who died young

Long Theatre:
donors were Thomas J. Long and also Robert M. Long, of Walnut Creek, both former regents, and founders of Longs Drug Stores

DeMarcus Brown Studio Theater:
theatre arts department head and director of Pacific theater from 1924 to 1969

The Jeannette Powell
Art Center (adjoining
new Geo-Sciences Center):
by Jeannette and Robert Powell of Sacramento. Among others, donors include, from Stockton, Grace Baun and the McClure family of Union Planing Mill

Benerd School of Education:
for Gladys Benerd, generous Pacific benefactor, opponent of smoking and other non-healthy habits, teacher at Stockton College

Olson Hall:
for the Olson family from Winifed Olson Raney

McGeorge School of Law campus: Sacramento

George Fuller Hall, the law lab:
named for a major donor and Sacramento businessman

Gordon D. Schaber Law Library:
for the dean who led the law school so productively from 1957 to 1992. Dean Schaber died in 1997.

Gary V. Schaber Student Center:
named for Gordon Schaber's younger brother, who served as associate dean for administration and died in 1981

Halbert House:
contains services for buildings, grounds, and maintenance; named for Mr. Sherrill Halbert, a federal judge, who made many contributions to McGeorge and Pacific

The Raymond Burr Lounge,
located in the California
Reading Room:
an avid supporter of the law school, the famed movie and television star contributed monetary gifts, art, books, and many scripts of *Perry Mason* and *Ironside*

University of the Pacific Dental School: San Francisco

The Hutto Patterson
Pediatric Clinic:
from Mrs. Clare Hutto of southern California through the Hutto Patterson Foundation

Molinari Pavilion:
from generous benefactor Arthur Molinari of Marin County, in honor of his family